Silence Amidst The Storm

Report On the Arab States' Positions Regarding
Israeli War In Gaza

GEW Reports & Analyses Team

Global East-West

Contents

Chapter 1

Introduction

T he Israeli-Palestinian conflict is one of the most contentious and long-standing disputes in modern history. As a famous writer and observer of global events, I have dedicated my efforts to unravelling the complexities of this conflict and shedding light on the various dimensions that influence it. In this book, I aim to provide a comprehensive analysis of the role Arab states play in the Israeli-Palestinian conflict, particularly focusing on their involvement in the recent Gaza War.

To understand the Israeli-Palestinian conflict in its entirety, it is crucial to delve into its historical context. The roots of this conflict can be traced back to the late 19th century, when a wave of Jewish migration to Palestine, driven by the Zionist movement, collided with the aspirations of the Arab population already living there. The clash of national identities and claims to the same land ignited tensions that continue to this day.

The conflict further intensified with the establishment of the state of Israel in 1948, following the United Nations partition plan which aimed to divide Palestine into separate Jewish and Arab states. Arab states vehemently rejected this plan, viewing it as an infringement on Arab sovereignty and an injustice towards the Palestinian people. As a result, they launched a military intervention to support the Palestinians, yet ultimately experienced defeat against the newly established Israeli forces. This led to the displacement of a significant number of Palestinian refugees and the occupation of the West Bank, the Gaza Strip, and East Jerusalem by Israel.

Arab states, due to their geographical proximity and historical ties, have been deeply involved in the Israeli-Palestinian conflict since its inception. One key aspect to consider is the Palestinian refugee issue, which has been a central concern for many Arab states. The influx of Palestinian refugees into neighbouring Arab countries has placed significant strains on their resources and stability. The sense of kinship and shared Arab identity has led many of these states to advocate for Palestinian rights and self-determination.

However, the involvement of Arab states in the Israeli-Palestinian conflict is not without its challenges and contradictions. While some Arab states, like Jordan and Egypt, have successfully signed peace agreements with Israel, others have maintained a steadfast stance against normalisation of relations until a just and lasting solution for the Palestinians is achieved.

The Arab League, established in 1945, has played a significant role in coordinating the efforts of Arab states regarding the Israeli-Palestinian conflict. Through various resolutions and diplomatic initiatives, the Arab League has consistently affirmed its support for the Palestinian cause, emphasising the need for Israeli withdrawal from occupied territories, the establishment of a Palestinian state, and the recognition of East Jerusalem as its capital. Arab states have been active participants within the league, employing a collective approach to address the conflict and advocate for Palestinian rights.

Additionally, the complex and varied nature of governance in the Arab world also plays a significant role in shaping their involvement in the

Israeli-Palestinian conflict. Some states have authoritarian governments that prioritise other national interests over the Palestinian cause. Instances of political unrest and domestic instability divert attention and resources away from the conflict. Moreover, regional rivalries and power struggles, such as the divide between Saudi Arabia and Iran, influence Arab states' positions on the Israeli-Palestinian conflict. These rivalries often result in divided alliances and further complicate the ability of Arab states to present a united front.

In recent years, the Gaza Strip has emerged as a focal point in the Israeli-Palestinian conflict, with the territory frequently subjected to military operations and siege by Israel. The recent Gaza War, which erupted in May 2021, brought the conflict to the forefront of international attention once again. Arab states, cognisant of their historical responsibility and to varying degrees, joined the international community in expressing concern and calling for an immediate ceasefire.

The role of Arab states in the recent Gaza War was multifaceted. Some Arab states, such as Egypt, played a significant diplomatic role in mediating a ceasefire between Israel and Palestinian factions in Gaza. Egypt's close geographic proximity to the Gaza Strip and historical ties with both Israel and Palestine made it an ideal mediator in this conflict. Through diplomatic channels, Egypt engaged in shuttle diplomacy, conducting intensive negotiations with all parties involved to deescalate the situation and reach a ceasefire agreement.

Other Arab states, such as Qatar and Turkey, took a more vocal and assertive stance in support of the Palestinians. These states provided financial aid, humanitarian assistance, and political backing to the Palestinians in Gaza. Qatar, in particular, has been actively involved in reconstruction efforts in Gaza, aiming to alleviate the dire living conditions resulting from the destruction caused by the conflict. Qatar's support, coupled with its influence on Hamas, the ruling authority in Gaza, has contributed to its significance in the Israeli-Palestinian conflict.

However, not all Arab states shared the same level of commitment and engagement. Some Arab states, particularly those with close ties to the United States, adopted a more cautious approach, urging restraint and advocating for a negotiated settlement rather than overtly supporting one side or the other. The Gulf Cooperation Council (GCC) states, such as Saudi Arabia and the United Arab Emirates, prioritised stability and regional cooperation, while also expressing support for the Palestinians and condemning Israeli actions in Gaza.

In conclusion, the Israeli-Palestinian conflict is a complex and deeply rooted issue, with the involvement of Arab states playing a significant role in shaping its trajectory. The historical context, shared Arab identity, and regional dynamics contribute to the complexities of Arab states' involvement in the conflict. The recent Gaza War highlighted the diverse approaches and challenges faced by Arab states as they navigate their national interests, balance regional alliances, and strive for a just and lasting resolution to the conflict. By examining the specific situations and motivations of each state, we can better understand the broader regional dynamics and identify the obstacles that hinder progress towards peace in the Israeli-Palestinian conflict.

Chapter 2

Understanding the Historical Context of the Israeli-Palestinian Conflict

The Israeli-Palestinian conflict is a deeply entrenched and intricate issue that spans decades, with its origins tracing back to the early 20th century. To fully comprehend the conflict, one must delve into its historical context, which includes a variety of factors such as the Zionist Movement, British colonisation, Arab nationalism, and the creation of the State of Israel.

At the heart of the conflict lies the Zionist Movement, which emerged in the late 19th century as a response to growing anti-Semitism in Europe. The movement aimed to establish a homeland for the Jewish people in Palestine, a land historically seen as sacred to both Judaism and Islam. The early pioneers of the Zionist Movement, led by figures like Theodor Herzl, believed that the establishment of a Jewish state was essential for the survival and freedom of persecuted Jews.

The World Zionist Organisation, founded in 1897, played a significant role in mobilising Jewish support for the Zionist cause and promoting Jewish immigration to Palestine. Jewish communities in Europe and around the world offered financial and political support, while Jewish settlement organisations purchased land from absentee Arab landlords, often at high prices, to establish agricultural communities.

The increase in Jewish immigration to Palestine, backed by the Zionist Movement, ultimately resulted in heightened tensions between the Jewish and Arab communities. The gradual eviction of Arab tenants and the encroachment on Arab lands fostered a feeling of dispossession and resentment among the Arab populace. In response, Arab nationalism emerged, with figures such as Haj Amin al-Husseini, the grand mufti of Jerusalem, advocating for the defence of Arab rights and opposing further Jewish immigration. Following World War I and the collapse of the Ottoman Empire, the League of Nations issued the Balfour Declaration in 1917, expressing support for the establishment in Palestine of a national home for the Jewish people. This declaration marked a pivotal moment for Zionism and laid the groundwork for Jewish immigration and eventually Israel's establishment.

The British Mandate for Palestine, granted by the League of Nations in 1922, further complicated matters. While aiming to facilitate a Jewish homeland, it also acknowledged the rights of the Arab majority. With conflicting commitments to both Jews and Arabs, the British administration encountered significant challenges in managing escalating tensions between these two communities.

British policies, such as the White Paper of 1939, further restricted Jewish immigration in response to Arab unrest, leading to resentment from Zionist leaders and increased Jewish paramilitary activities against the Arab population. Groups like the Irgun and Lehi carried out attacks on both

British forces and Arab civilians, seeking to remove British control and establish a Jewish state.

In parallel, Arab nationalism continued to grow stronger, fuelled by anti-colonial sentiments and a desire for self-determination among the Arab population. The Arab Higher Committee, led by prominent figures such as Haj Amin al-Husseini and Awni Abd al-Hadi, sought Arab unity and independence, rejecting any compromise that would lead to the establishment of a Jewish state.

Despite the escalating tensions, Jewish immigration continued to increase throughout the 1930s and 1940s, as Holocaust survivors and dispossessed Jewish refugees sought refuge in Palestine. The Jewish community established its own institutions, such as the Haganah defence force, the Jewish Agency for Palestine, and various paramilitary groups, all aimed at protecting Jewish settlers and promoting Zionist goals.

The Holocaust, which occurred during World War II, further underscored the urgency of establishing a Jewish homeland. The scale of the Holocaust and the atrocities committed against Jews by Nazi Germany, along with the international community's failure to protect them, undoubtedly shaped global sympathy and support for the Zionist cause.

The 1947 United Nations Partition Plan for Palestine, which proposed the division of Palestine into separate Jewish and Arab states with an internationalised Jerusalem, was accepted by Jewish leaders but vehemently rejected by Arab states and Palestinian leadership. Jewish leaders saw it as a step towards achieving their aspirations, while Arab nations believed it disregarded the will of the majority Arab population.

The rejection of the partition plan by Arab states led to a full-scale war after the State of Israel was proclaimed in 1948. Arab states, including

Jordan, Egypt, Syria, and Iraq, intervened to support the Palestinians, viewing the establishment of Israel as a threat to their own stability and pan-Arab aspirations. The resulting 1948 Arab-Israeli War, also known as the War of Independence or Nakba (Catastrophe) from the Palestinian perspective, resulted in the displacement of hundreds of thousands of Palestinians. Approximately 700,000 Palestinians became refugees, either fleeing or being expelled from their homes during the war. This event is a deeply ingrained memory in Palestinian collective consciousness and a major source of contention in the conflict.

The conflict has continued for decades, marked by numerous wars, uprisings, and attempts at peace. The Six-Day War in 1967, triggered by escalating tensions between Israel and neighbouring Arab states, resulted in Israel's occupation of the West Bank, Gaza Strip, and East Jerusalem, further intensifying Palestinian demands for self-determination and fuelling Palestinian resistance movements such as the Palestine Liberation Organisation (PLO) and later Hamas.

The Oslo Accords in the 1990s, signed between Israel and the PLO, initiated a peace process aimed at achieving a two-state solution. However, the failure to fully implement the agreements, ongoing Israeli settlements in the occupied territories, and the lack of progress in resolving key issues like the status of Jerusalem and the right of return for Palestinian refugees have hindered peace efforts. These unresolved issues, along with divisions and disagreements within both societies, have perpetuated the cycle of violence, distrust, and lack of progress in resolving the Israeli-Palestinian conflict.

Understanding the historical context of the Israeli-Palestinian conflict is crucial to grasping the complexities and challenges involved in resolving the ongoing disputes. It requires acknowledging the intertwined narratives, aspirations, and grievances of both Israelis and Palestinians, as well as the influence of external actors and geopolitical dynamics. Only through a comprehensive understanding can meaningful steps be taken towards achieving just and lasting peace in the region.

Chapter 3

Exploring the 21 Arab States and Their Individual Stances on the Gaza War

In exploring the 21 Arab states and their individual stances on the Gaza War, it is crucial to delve even deeper into the complex motivations, historical backgrounds, and political dynamics that shape their positions. As the Israeli-Palestinian conflict persists, regional actors navigate their relationships with both sides, balance their national interests, and engage with the broader international community. Each Arab state brings its own unique set of concerns, interests, and challenges to the table, further shaping the diverse perspectives evident in this chapter.

Algeria, with its revolutionary history and longstanding support for anti-colonial struggles, has been a strong advocate for the Palestinian cause. The Algerian government views the Israeli occupation of Palestinian ter-

ritories as a grave violation of international law and calls for the implementation of relevant United Nations resolutions, including the right of
return for Palestinian refugees. Algeria has not only provided financial
and diplomatic support to Palestine but also served as a hub for political and intellectual solidarity with the Palestinian cause. The Algerian
National Liberation Front (FLN), which fought against French colonial
rule, inspired other nationalist liberation movements, and there is a sense
of shared struggle and empathy between Algeria and Palestine. Algerian
leaders have consistently condemned Israeli actions and called for an immediate end to the blockade and the restoration of basic humanitarian
conditions in Gaza.

Bahrain, located in the Persian Gulf, presents a more complex stance
due to its close ties with Saudi Arabia and the United Arab Emirates
(UAE). While expressing concern for the suffering of Palestinians in Gaza,
Bahrain has adopted a more cautious approach in asserting its position. The Bahraini government's fear of antagonising its powerful neighbours and destabilising the region has influenced its involvement in the
Gaza War.
Bahrain has historically been aligned with Saudi Arabia and, more recently,
the UAE, as part of a regional alliance aiming to counter Iranian influence
in the Gulf.

These geopolitical dynamics and security concerns have led Bahrain to
maintain a more muted public stance on the conflict. However, Bahrain
has attempted to strike a balance by simultaneously expressing solidarity
with the Palestinian cause and supporting diplomatic efforts towards a
peaceful resolution.

Comoros, a small island nation in the Indian Ocean, grapples with numerous challenges in engaging with the Gaza War. As a member of the

Arab League, Comoros has participated in joint efforts to address the crisis. However, the country's limited resources, geopolitical challenges, and internal socio-economic concerns have hindered its ability to actively contribute to resolving the conflict. The Comorian government expresses solidarity with the Palestinian people and their right to self-determination. Despite its limited capacity to influence the conflict directly, Comoros has made efforts to support the Palestinian cause diplomatically, including through engaging with international forums and advocating for a just and lasting resolution to the Israeli-Palestinian conflict.

Djibouti, situated in the strategic Horn of Africa, faces its own set of challenges in navigating the Gaza War. The country relies heavily on foreign aid and depends on its strategic location as a key transit hub for international trade and military operations. Engaging more visibly in the conflict could potentially jeopardise its financial resources, regional stability, and its vital role in providing military bases to foreign powers. Despite these constraints, Djibouti has expressed solidarity with the Palestinian cause and called for an immediate end to the violence. The Djiboutian government has urged the international community to address the underlying issues driving the conflict, emphasising the need for a just and lasting solution that upholds Palestinian rights.

Egypt, historically intertwined with the Israeli-Palestinian conflict, plays a pivotal and multifaceted role in shaping regional dynamics. The Camp David Accords of 1978, which led to the normalisation of Egypt-Israel relations, introduced a complex dynamic into the equation.

While maintaining a peace treaty with Israel, Egypt has committed significant efforts to mediating conflicts, including the Gaza War.

Egypt's objective has been to restore calm and facilitate negotiations between Israel and Hamas, the governing authority in Gaza. However, the country faces the constant challenge of balancing its relationship with Israel, managing domestic anti-Israel sentiments, addressing the needs and aspirations of its own population, and protecting its national security interests in the Sinai Peninsula. These factors significantly impact Egypt's stance on the Gaza War and its role in brokering ceasefire agreements and facilitating humanitarian assistance to the Palestinian people.

Iraq, emerging from years of conflict and still grappling with internal struggles and security concerns, focuses primarily on ensuring its own stability and combating terrorism within its borders. The country's focus on post-conflict reconstruction and maintaining its territorial integrity limits Iraq's capacity to exert significant influence on the Israeli-Palestinian conflict. However, Iraq has consistently voiced support for the Palestinian cause, calling for an end to the Israeli occupation and the establishment of an independent Palestinian state. Iraq's engagement in the conflict primarily takes the form of political support, diplomatic efforts, and advocating for international resolutions that align with its vision for a just resolution.

Jordan, a country that has historically played a key role in the peace process and hosts a significant number of Palestinian refugees, is confronted with unique pressures and constraints in relation to the Gaza War. Jordan's close geographic proximity to the Palestinian territories and its deep historical ties to the Palestinian cause shape its approach to the conflict. The country faces the risk of spillover violence and popular unrest resulting from the Israeli-Palestinian conflict. Jordan has historically navigated a cautious path, engaging diplomatically, advocating for a two-state solution, and encouraging international mediation efforts.

However, Jordan's stance also considers its own national security interests, its relationship with Israel, and the need to maintain stability amidst regional political turbulence.

Kuwait, another country deeply connected to the Palestinian issue, has faced its own set of challenges in supporting Palestine. Kuwait has a well-established tradition of supporting Palestinian rights and providing significant financial aid to Palestine, particularly to support reconstruction efforts in the aftermath of conflicts. However, internal political dynamics, the pressure to maintain a neutral regional position, and its reliance on foreign labour have limited Kuwait's direct involvement in the conflict. Nevertheless, Kuwait has remained vocal in condemning Israeli actions, calling for the protection of Palestinian rights, and urging the international community to take stronger measures to end the violence. Kuwait also contributes to the financing of United Nations relief and humanitarian programmes in Palestine.

Lebanon, with its complex sectarian and political landscape, struggles to maintain a unified stance on the Gaza War.

The country hosts a large number of Palestinian refugees, who constitute a significant portion of its population, and has experienced conflicts related to Palestinian factions.

These internal dynamics have made it challenging for Lebanon to assert a cohesive position on the conflict. The Lebanese government has historically supported the Palestinian cause and called for an end to the Israeli occupation, pushing for international resolutions that uphold Palestinian self-determination. However, Lebanon's delicate power-sharing arrangements, the influence of political parties associated with various Palestinian factions, and the sensitivity surrounding Lebanon's relationship with Israel shape its approach to the conflict.

Lebanon has also been severely impacted by the spillover effects of regional conflicts, such as the Syrian civil war, further complicating its engagement in the Israeli-Palestinian conflict.

Libya, torn by internal strife and ongoing power struggles, faces major obstacles in exerting significant influence on the Gaza War. Since the fall of Muammar Gaddafi's regime in 2011, Libya has been embroiled in a protracted civil conflict, with multiple factions vying for control. As a result, the country has struggled to address its own internal challenges, including ensuring stability, combating terrorism, and establishing a functioning government. These domestic priorities have limited Libya's capacity to actively engage in the Israeli-Palestinian conflict. However, Libya has historically supported the Palestinian cause and the right to self-determination, calling for an end to the Israeli occupation and the establishment of an independent Palestinian state. Despite its limited influence, Libya has used its platform in international organisations, such as the Arab League and the United Nations, to advocate for the Palestinian cause and condemn Israeli actions.

Mauritania, a West African nation with cultural and historical ties to the Arab world, faces its own unique challenges and limitations in engaging with the Gaza War. As a member of the Arab League, Mauritania has demonstrated solidarity with Palestine and condemned Israeli actions. However, the country's geographic distance, limited resources, and internal development priorities diminish its direct influence on the conflict. Mauritania's focus is primarily on addressing its socioeconomic challenges, promoting stability, and advancing regional integration in West Africa. Nevertheless, Mauritania has consistently called for an end to the Israeli occupation, the preservation of Palestinian rights, and the establishment of an independent Palestinian state.

Morocco, while not directly involved in the Gaza War due to its geographic location, has a longstanding commitment to the Palestinian cause and the pursuit of a just and lasting solution. Morocco's history as a key player in the Arab-Israeli conflict, its hosting of several rounds of peace negotiations, and its recognition of the Palestinian Liberation Organisation (PLO) in the early 1980s have contributed to its influential role in the region. The Moroccan government has consistently expressed solidarity with the Palestinian people and their right to self-determination, advocating for an end to the Israeli occupation, and supporting efforts to achieve a two-state solution. Morocco has used its diplomatic channels, multilateral forums, and economic assistance to advance the Palestinian cause and contribute to the stability of the region.

Oman, known for its policy of non-interference and neutrality in regional conflicts, maintains a cautious stance in the Gaza War. The Sultanate has historically advocated for a peaceful resolution to the Israeli-Palestinian conflict and supported the Palestinian cause. Oman has consistently called for the establishment of an independent Palestinian state based on the 1967 borders and the right of return for Palestinian refugees. However, its focus on maintaining good relations with regional and international actors, promoting stability in the Gulf, and preserving its neutrality shape Oman's approach to the conflict. Oman prefers to play a behind-the-scenes role, supporting diplomatic efforts and facilitating dialogue, rather than taking a more overt position.

Qatar, a regional player known for its assertive foreign policy, has played a significant role in the Israeli-Palestinian conflict. Qatar has been a consistent supporter of the Palestinian cause and has provided substantial financial aid to Palestine. The Qatari government views the Israeli occupation as a violation of international law and has called for the establishment of an independent Palestinian state. Qatar has used its extensive media network, Al Jazeera, to raise awareness about the plight of Palestinians and highlight the injustices committed against them. Qatar has also hosted several rounds of peace negotiations, facilitated reconciliation talks, and mediated ceasefire agreements between Israel and Hamas.

Saudi Arabia, as the custodian of Islam's holiest sites and one of the most influential countries in the Arab world, holds a crucial role in the Israeli-Palestinian conflict. Saudi Arabia has historically called for an end to the Israeli occupation, the establishment of an independent Palestinian state, and the protection of Palestinian rights. However, Saudi Arabia's position is often complicated by its strategic alliance with the United States and shared interests on regional security issues. The Kingdom has prioritised its relationship with the US and regional stability, which have at times influenced its public posture on the conflict. Saudi Arabia has played a significant role in supporting Palestine financially, providing aid to Palestinians and supporting reconstruction efforts. It has also engaged in diplomatic efforts to promote reconciliation and facilitate dialogue between Palestinian factions.

Sudan, emerging from a long period of internal conflict and undergoing a delicate political transition, faces numerous challenges in engaging with the Gaza War. The Sudanese government has expressed solidarity with the Palestinian people and their right to an independent state. However, Sudan is focused on addressing its internal challenges, such as the establishment of a democratic system and resolving conflicts between various factions. Sudan's domestic priorities limit its capacity to exert significant influence on the Israeli-Palestinian conflict. Nevertheless, Sudan has historically supported Palestinian rights and advocated for an end to the Israeli occupation.

Syria, embroiled in a devastating civil war since 2011, has been preoccupied with internal conflict and addressing its own security concerns. The Syrian government has historically positioned itself as a strong supporter of the Palestinian cause and has called for an end to the Israeli occupation. However, the ongoing civil war has significantly disrupted Syria's ability to project influence and contribute to the resolution of the Israeli-Palestinian conflict. The government's focus has been on maintaining its own survival, countering opposition forces, and securing its territory. The conflict in Syria has also exacerbated regional tensions and created a fragmented landscape that impacts its engagement in the broader Arab-Israeli conflict.

Tunisia, the birthplace of the Arab Spring and a country undergoing its own political transition, faces a delicate balance in engaging with the Gaza War. Tunisia has historically been supportive of the Palestinian cause, calling for an end to the Israeli occupation and the establishment of an independent Palestinian state. However, Tunisia also confronts internal challenges, such as democratic consolidation, economic development, and security concerns. These priorities shape Tunisia's approach to the conflict, with a focus on advocating for Palestinian rights through diplomatic channels and supporting international resolutions that promote a just and lasting solution.

The United Arab Emirates (UAE), a key player in regional politics and a close ally of the United States, is cautious in its approach to the Gaza War. The UAE historically maintained a neutral position on the Israeli-Palestinian conflict, prioritising its relationship with the US and regional stability. However, recent developments, including the signing of the Abraham Accords, have led to a normalisation of relations between Israel and the UAE. This shift in dynamics has influenced the UAE's public stance on the conflict, with a more nuanced approach aimed at supporting diplomatic efforts and advancing regional cooperation. The UAE has also provided financial aid for reconstruction in Gaza and engaged in humanitarian efforts to alleviate the suffering of the Palestinian people.

Yemen, mired in a protracted civil war and grappling with a humanitarian catastrophe, faces severe limitations and challenges in engaging with the Gaza War. The Yemeni government has expressed solidarity with the Palestinian cause, called for an end to the Israeli occupation, and supported

Palestinian rights. However, the country's focus is primarily on resolving its own internal conflict, addressing the humanitarian crisis, and securing its territory. The war in Yemen has created a fragmented and deeply divided landscape that hinders its ability to play a significant role in the Israeli-Palestinian conflict. Yemen's engagement primarily takes the form of political support and diplomatic efforts within regional and international forums.

In conclusion, the Arab states' positions on the Gaza War are shaped by a complex web of historical, political, and geopolitical factors. While there are commonalities in their support for the Palestinian cause, each state also brings its unique concerns, interests, and challenges to the table. From Algeria's revolutionary history to Jordan's geographic proximity to the Palestinian territories and political stability, each country's approach to the Gaza War reflects its own internal dynamics and external relations. Despite their varying levels of influence and engagement, the Arab states play a critical role in raising international awareness about the plight of the Palestinian people, advocating for their rights, and supporting efforts towards a just and lasting solution to the Israeli-Palestinian conflict. While the Arab states' effectiveness in influencing the outcome of the Gaza War may vary, their collective voice and support for Palestine contribute to the broader regional and international discourse on the conflict.

Chapter 4

Algeria's Role and Challenges in Achieving a Cease-fire

A lgeria has long been involved in attempts to find a resolution to the Israeli-Palestinian conflict and has played a crucial role in facilitating peace negotiations. However, achieving a cease-fire between Israel and Palestine has posed significant challenges for Algeria due to a myriad of complex factors.

One of the main challenges Algeria faces is the deep-rooted animosity between the two parties involved in the conflict. The Israeli-Palestinian conflict traces its origins back to the early 20th century, marked by competing claims to the land and historical narratives that have deep emotional and symbolic significance for both Israelis and Palestinians. This prolonged conflict has resulted in generations entrenched in narratives of victimhood, territorial disputes, and competing national aspirations. Consequently, this has created an immense barrier to communication and reconciliation, making it difficult for Algeria, and other mediators, to foster dialogue and establish common ground for negotiations.

Furthermore, the geopolitical dynamics in the region add to the complexities faced by Algeria. The Israeli-Palestinian conflict is not isolated but rather intertwined with broader regional and international dynamics. External powers, such as the United States, Russia, and the European Union, have often played significant roles in influencing the course of negotiations, advancing their own interests, and agendas. These external actors have historically invested in the region for political, economic, and security reasons, keen to exert their influence over the peace process. Additionally, regional actors like Iran, Saudi Arabia, and Turkey have used the Israeli-Palestinian conflict as a proxy for their own rivalries and ambitions, further complicating the path to a cease-fire. Algeria finds itself navigating this intricate web of regional and international interests, seeking to maintain its impartial stance while advancing the cause of peace.

Another challenge for Algeria is the internal fragmentation within the Palestinian leadership. With numerous political factions and groups vying for power and influence, the Palestinian side often lacks a unified voice in negotiations. Fatah, the dominant party in the Palestinian Authority, and Hamas, the Islamic resistance movement controlling the Gaza Strip, have historically held diverging approaches and strategies towards achieving Palestinian statehood. Such divisions have led to political infighting, weakened coherent leadership, and created internal tensions that hinder sustained progress towards a negotiated settlement. However, Algeria recognises the importance of bridging these internal divisions and believes that a unified Palestinian front is crucial for successful negotiations.

Additionally, the socio-economic conditions in both Israel and Palestine play a crucial role in the success or failure of cease-fire negotiations. In Palestine, the high levels of poverty, unemployment, and limited access to basic services exacerbate tensions and create a volatile environment.

The continued presence of Israeli settlements in the West Bank, checkpoints, and restricted movement further fuel Palestinian grievances. The dire socio-economic situation endured by Palestinians amplifies their frustrations and undermines the prospects for peace. Similarly, the economic disparities within Israeli society, particularly between Israeli Jews and Arab citizens, contribute to a sense of inequality and deepen existing grievances. Addressing these underlying socio-economic factors is essential for any comprehensive and sustainable cease-fire agreement.

Despite these challenges, Algeria remains committed to pursuing a peaceful resolution to the Israeli-Palestinian conflict. The country has actively participated in diplomatic initiatives, hosted peace conferences, and provided financial support to Palestinian institutions and humanitarian causes over the years. Known for its non-aligned position and diplomatic strength, Algeria strives to strike a delicate balance between the demands and aspirations of both parties, seeking common ground while upholding the principles of justice and international law.

Algeria firmly believes that a just and lasting peace can only be achieved through dialogue, respect for international law, and the rights of all parties involved. The country continues to advocate for a two-state solution, with Israel and Palestine coexisting side by side in peace and security. As Algeria navigates the challenges posed by deep-seated animosities, external interventions, political fragmentation, and socio-economic hardships, it will persist in its efforts to forge a path towards a comprehensive and enduring cease-fire, ultimately bringing an end to the long-standing Israeli-Palestinian conflict. Algeria's unwavering commitment to peace serves as a testament to the resilience and determination required to overcome the thorny issues at hand and build a future of coexistence and prosperity for both Israelis and Palestinians.

Chapter 5

Bahrain's Position and the Obstacles to Resolving the Conflict

Bahrain, a small island nation located in the Persian Gulf, has garnered significant prominence and recognition for its stance on the Israeli-Palestinian conflict. As a proud member of the Arab League and the Gulf Cooperation Council, Bahrain has consistently demonstrated unwavering support for the Palestinian cause and advocated for the establishment of an independent Palestinian state.

However, Bahrain faces numerous intricate obstacles when it comes to actively contributing to the resolution of this enduring and complex conflict. One of the significant challenges lies in the delicate balancing act it must perform due to its close relationship with the United States. Hosting the U.S. Navy's Fifth Fleet and maintaining a longstanding security partnership with the United States, Bahrain finds itself in a position where it must delicately balance its support for the Palestinians with the necessity of maintaining robust ties with its American allies. Consequently, Bahrain often finds its ability to take tangible actions that could potentially impact its relationship with the United States severely restricted.

Bahrain's strong relationship with the United States allows it to exert influence in diplomatic circles and engage in dialogue surrounding the Israeli-Palestinian conflict. However, it also means that Bahrain's actions must align with American interests and policies in the region, sometimes constraining its ability to robustly advocate for the Palestinians. Nonetheless, Bahrain has utilised its relationship with the United States to encourage dialogue between all parties involved and promote peaceful negotiations.

Another pivotal obstacle Bahrain encounters revolves around its internal politics. The country has experienced its own share of internal tensions, particularly between its Shia majority population and the Sunni ruling elite. These tensions have been exacerbated by regional rivalries, such as the rivalry between Saudi Arabia and Iran, which have influenced Bahrain's internal dynamics. Criticism from international entities regarding the government's suppression of dissent and the crackdown on opposition groups has further complicated Bahrain's ability to engage proactively in the Israeli-Palestinian issue without inviting scrutiny from the global community and human rights organisations.

The internal predicament places Bahrain in a challenging position, as it must navigate its commitment to the Palestinian cause while grappling with its own domestic challenges. Nevertheless, Bahrain has taken steps toward addressing these challenges, such as initiating political reforms and engaging in dialogue with different segments of society, aiming to foster greater inclusivity and participation.

Furthermore, Bahrain's geographical proximity to Saudi Arabia presents yet another set of hurdles. As a major regional power, Saudi Arabia carries substantial influence in the Middle East and has long-held its own steadfast stance on the Israeli-Palestinian conflict. Bahrain, being located in such close proximity to Saudi Arabia, must cautiously manoeuvre its relationship with this regional heavyweight, as any moves that run counter to Saudi Arabia's position may lead to strained relations between the two countries.

Despite these formidable obstacles, Bahrain continues to make earnest efforts to directly contribute to the resolution of the Israeli-Palestinian conflict. The nation actively participates in various regional and international initiatives that aim to find a peaceful and just solution to this longstanding dispute. Bahrain's call for the revival of the Arab Peace Initiative serves as a testament to its commitment to peace in the region. This initiative outlines a comprehensive framework for peace between Israel and the Arab world, with a significant emphasis on the establishment of a sovereign Palestinian state with East Jerusalem as its capital.

Bahrain's involvement in international forums allows it to articulate the aspirations of the Arab world and advocate for the rights of the Palestinian people. It has consistently emphasised the need for a just and lasting solution that ensures the rights and self-determination of the Palestinians, while also recognising the right of Israel to exist in peace and security.

In conclusion, Bahrain's position on the Israeli-Palestinian conflict is rooted in a firm commitment to the Palestinian cause and a steadfast desire for a just and enduring peace. However, the nation confronts multifaceted roadblocks, including navigating its close ties with the United States, managing its internal political challenges, and carefully manoeuvring regional dynamics. Nevertheless, Bahrain remains resolute in playing its part, albeit with limitations, towards resolving the Israeli-Palestinian conflict and supporting the definitive establishment of a Palestinian state. Through diplomatic initiatives, engagement in international forums, and domestic reforms, Bahrain strives to contribute to a peaceful and prosperous future for the region.

Chapter 6

Comoros' Dilemma and Its Impact on the Palestinian Struggle

Comoros, a small archipelago located off the eastern coast of Africa, faces numerous internal challenges that pose significant obstacles to its ability to effectively support the Palestinian struggle. Situated in a region where geopolitical tensions run high, Comoros finds itself torn between domestic issues and its desire to contribute to the resolution of the Israeli-Palestinian conflict.

One of Comoros' primary dilemmas is its weak economy and limited resources. As a developing nation, the archipelago grapples with considerable socio-economic challenges. High poverty rates and limited infrastructure development demand significant attention and investment from the Comorian government. The majority of the population relies on subsistence farming and fishing, leading to vulnerability to climate change and the volatility of global commodity markets. These domestic issues leave Comoros with little capacity to allocate resources and funds towards supporting the Palestinian cause.

Furthermore, Comoros' geographical location in the Indian Ocean shapes its domestic concerns and foreign policy priorities. The archipelago's vulnerability to natural disasters such as cyclones and earthquakes further diverts resources and attention away from external affairs. Comoros must focus on disaster preparedness and response mechanisms to safeguard its own populace, limiting its ability to extend considerable support to external causes, including Palestine.

Consequently, the limited financial resources available to Comoros restrict its ability to engage in meaningful initiatives that could assist the Palestinian struggle. The archipelago's budget constraints make it difficult to provide substantial financial aid or contribute to diplomatic efforts aimed at resolving the conflict. Comoros must prioritise its own economic advancement and development initiatives before extending significant support to external causes.

Moreover, Comoros faces challenges in attracting foreign investment and promoting economic growth. The archipelago lacks a diversified economic base, heavily relying on agriculture and fishing sectors. The absence of a strong industrial and service sector limits the opportunities for economic expansion and reduces the capacity to generate additional revenue. Comoros needs to prioritise its economic development to alleviate poverty and create job opportunities.

Comoros' historical ties with Arab countries also play a role in its approach to the Palestinian struggle. The archipelago shares cultural and religious affinity with Arab nations that support Palestinian self-determination. Comoros has recognised the State of Palestine and has consistently voiced its support for Palestinian rights and statehood. However, due to its limited international influence, Comoros struggles to mobilise regional Arab support for the Palestinian cause effectively.

Additionally, Comoros' diplomatic capabilities are hindered by its small size and lack of international influence. Despite being a member of the United Nations and the African Union, Comoros often struggles to have its voice heard on the global stage. The archipelago's limited diplomatic footprint constrains its impact and limits its ability to actively participate in diplomatic initiatives aimed at resolving the Israeli-Palestinian conflict.

This lack of international influence also hampers Comoros' ability to mobilise regional and international support for the Palestinian cause. While the archipelago may hold firm positions on the issue and express solidarity with the Palestinian struggle, it can struggle to garner widespread support due to its limited diplomatic weight. Comoros relies heavily on regional and international partners for support and assistance, further restricting its ability to independently contribute to the resolution of the conflict.

Internal conflicts and political instability within Comoros further compound its dilemma. Like many other nations in the region, the archipelago is grappling with internal power struggles and frequent changes in leadership. These internal conflicts divert attention and resources away from external affairs, making it even more challenging for Comoros to provide consistent and focused support to the Palestinian struggle.

Despite these challenges, Comoros has made efforts to express solidarity with the Palestinian cause. The nation has repeatedly condemned Israeli actions in the Occupied Palestinian Territories and has called for a peaceful resolution to the conflict based on international law and the recognition of Palestinian statehood. Comoros has also extended humanitarian aid and support to Palestine, although on a relatively small scale.

In conclusion, Comoros faces a complex dilemma when it comes to supporting the Palestinian struggle. Internal challenges, including a weak economy, limited resources, vulnerability to natural disasters, and political instability, hinder Comoros' ability to actively engage in diplomatic efforts and provide substantial support to Palestine. Despite expressing solidarity and offering limited aid, Comoros' impact on the Palestinian struggle is constrained by its small size, limited international influence, and internal conflicts. The archipelago must navigate these challenges and work towards building stronger partnerships to enhance its contribution to the resolution of the Israeli-Palestinian conflict.

Chapter 7

Djibouti's Involvement and the Barriers to Peace

Djibouti, a small nation located on the Horn of Africa, has played a role in the Israeli-Palestinian conflict, albeit with limited influence. Despite its geographical proximity to the conflict zone, Djibouti faces several barriers in actively participating in the peace process.

One of the primary barriers is the nation's size and limited resources. Djibouti's small population of just under one million people poses challenges in allocating significant resources towards international engagements. Its economy heavily relies on port services, which limits its capacity to mobilise the necessary financial and logistical support required for extensive involvement in the Israeli-Palestinian conflict. Moreover, Djibouti faces high levels of poverty, unemployment, and a lack of infrastructure development. These internal concerns divert attention and resources away from external conflicts, making it difficult for Djibouti to dedicate significant efforts to mediating the Israeli-Palestinian conflict. Limited access to quality education and healthcare also diminishes Djibouti's ability to nurture a well-informed and empowered diplomatic corps.

Additionally, Djibouti's strategic positioning as a host to military bases of several global powers further inhibits its active involvement in conflict resolution efforts. The nation is strategically located at the junction of crucial trade routes, making it an attractive location for military installations for the United States, France, and China. Djibouti's stable political environment and security guarantee have played a significant role in attracting these global powers, which, in turn, contribute to its security, development, and foreign investment. This dual role of being a key regional military hub and a mediator in the Israeli-Palestinian conflict poses a delicate balancing act for Djibouti. The need to maintain favourable relationships with these powerful states often takes precedence over active involvement in the peace process.

Furthermore, Djibouti, like many other Arab states, faces pressure from regional dynamics that affect its position on the Israeli-Palestinian conflict. Historically, Djibouti has participated in pan-Arab initiatives and closely aligned its stance with the Arab League, which supports a two-state solution and recognises East Jerusalem as the capital of the future Palestinian state. However, Djibouti must also navigate the complexities of regional politics. Neighbouring countries like Saudi Arabia and Egypt exert influence and have significant geopolitical and economic interests in the region. Their positions often shape Djibouti's stance, as the nation seeks to maintain favourable relationships and navigate regional dynamics that may impact its own stability and security. Thus, Djibouti's independence in shaping the peace process is limited.

Despite these barriers, Djibouti has made efforts to contribute to the peace process by participating in international forums. The nation frequently raises the issue of the Israeli-Palestinian conflict in the United

Nations General Assembly, where it utilises its platform to voice support for Palestinian rights and advocate for a just solution to the conflict. Djibouti actively engages with international partners and regional stakeholders through diplomatic channels, expressing its commitment to peace and stability in the region.

Furthermore, Djibouti has provided humanitarian aid to Palestinians affected by the conflict. The country collaborates with international organisations to deliver medical supplies, food, and other essential items to those in need. Djibouti recognises the dire situation faced by Palestinians and acknowledges the responsibility of the international community in alleviating their suffering. As a gesture of solidarity, Djibouti extends support to those affected by the conflict, despite its own resource limitations.

In conclusion, Djibouti's involvement in the Israeli-Palestinian conflict is hindered by its limited resources, internal challenges, the delicate balancing act as a military hub, and the influence of regional dynamics. While Djibouti recognises the importance of a peaceful resolution and supports the Palestinian cause, its ability to actively participate in conflict resolution efforts remains constrained. Nonetheless, the nation continues to express its support through diplomatic avenues, international forums, and humanitarian aid contributions, seeking to contribute within the limits of its capacity. Djibouti's commitment to peace serves as a reminder that even small nations with limited resources can play a vital role in advocating for a just and lasting resolution to the Israeli-Palestinian conflict.

Chapter 8

Egypt's Complex Relationship with Palestine and Israel

Egypt has played a significant role in the Israeli-Palestinian conflict due to its geographical proximity and historical ties to both sides. This chapter delves into the complex relationship that Egypt has had with Palestine and Israel, exploring the challenges and dynamics that have shaped their interactions.

Since the establishment of the State of Israel in 1948, Egypt has been intricately involved in the conflict. Initially, Egypt had a hostile relationship with Israel, considering it a threat to Arab unity and the Palestinian cause. This resulted in several wars between the two nations, such as the 1956 Suez Crisis, the Six-Day War in 1967, and the Yom Kippur War in 1973. These conflicts strained the relationship and created deep animosity and mistrust.

However, in recent decades, Egypt has adopted a more pragmatic approach towards the conflict, actively engaging in peace negotiations and diplomatic efforts. The signing of the Camp David Accords in 1978 between Egypt and Israel marked a significant turning point. Through this agreement, Egypt became the first Arab nation to officially recognise Israel as a sovereign state, and in return, Israel withdrew from the Sinai Peninsula.

This shift in Egypt's approach was driven by several factors. Firstly, Egypt recognised the need for stability in the region and saw diplomacy as the most viable way to achieve it. The devastation caused by the wars had taken a toll on both nations, and Egypt sought to prevent further loss of life and destruction. Secondly, Egypt sought to regain its leadership position in the Arab world, and brokering peace between Israel and Palestine was seen as a way to enhance its regional influence.

However, Egypt's relationship with Palestine has also been complex. While Egypt has historically supported the Palestinian cause and advocated for their rights, including their aspirations for statehood, it has at times faced criticism for its approach. Some Palestinians argue that Egypt has prioritised its own interests over the Palestinian struggle, particularly during periods of negotiations with Israel.

Additionally, Egypt has faced challenges in its efforts to broker peace between Israel and Palestine. The fragmentation within the Palestinian leadership, with the divided governance of the West Bank and the Gaza Strip, has complicated Egypt's role as a mediator. The internal disputes between Fatah and Hamas, the two major Palestinian political factions, have often hindered progress in achieving a united Palestinian front.

Moreover, Egypt has had to navigate the complexities of its relationship with Israel while balancing its commitments to the Arab street and the broader Arab world. Egypt's willingness to cooperate with Israel has sometimes led to criticism and accusations of betrayal from other Arab nations and the Palestinian population.

In recent years, Egypt has been actively involved in facilitating ceasefires and reconciliation efforts between Israel and Hamas, particularly during times of heightened hostilities in the Gaza Strip. Egypt's border crossing with Gaza, the Rafah border crossing, has served as a crucial lifeline for Palestinians, allowing for the movement of goods and people.

Furthermore, Egypt has utilised its regional influence to engage with other international actors to advance the Israeli-Palestinian peace process. It has participated in multilateral initiatives such as the Oslo Accords, the Madrid Conference, and more recently, the Arab Peace Initiative. These efforts have aimed to create a framework for negotiations, address the core issues of the conflict, and promote a just and comprehensive peace settlement.

Egypt's role as a mediator has often required delicate diplomacy and perseverance. It has utilised its longstanding relationships with various regional actors, such as the United States, the European Union, and Arab states, to garner support and foster dialogue between Israel and Palestine. Egypt has also facilitated indirect negotiations, bringing together Israeli and Palestinian representatives in Cairo to discuss ceasefires, prisoner exchanges, and other issues of mutual concern.

However, despite its efforts, Egypt has faced limitations in its ability to bring about a lasting peace between Israel and Palestine. The unresolved issues of borders, settlements, the status of Jerusalem, and the right of return for Palestinian refugees continue to pose significant obstacles to a comprehensive resolution. Furthermore, the lack of trust between the parties involved and the influence of hardline factions on both sides further complicate the peace process.

Egypt's relationship with Israel has experienced its share of challenges as well. While both nations have enjoyed periods of peaceful coexistence and cooperation, there have been instances of strained relations, such as Egypt's recall of its ambassador to Israel in 2012 following the Israeli military operation in Gaza. These incidents highlight the delicate nature of the relationship and the sensitivity of public opinion in both countries.

In its pursuit of peace, Egypt has also addressed the economic aspects of the conflict, recognising the importance of development and prosperity for long-term stability. The Egyptian government has actively supported projects aimed at improving the socioeconomic conditions of Palestinians, particularly in the Gaza Strip. Efforts have been made to enhance infrastructure, education, healthcare, and trade opportunities, and to create economic growth that benefits both Palestinians and Egyptians.

In conclusion, Egypt's relationship with Palestine and Israel is complex and multifaceted. While Egypt has shifted from a confrontational position towards one of diplomacy and peace negotiations, it faces challenges in balancing its interests with the demands and aspirations of the Palestinian people. The road to achieving a just and lasting resolution to the Israeli-Palestinian conflict is fraught with obstacles, but Egypt's engagement remains crucial in the pursuit of a peaceful solution. Through its diplomatic endeavours, mediation efforts, economic support, and regional influence, Egypt continues to shape the dynamics and seek opportunities for dialogue and reconciliation between Palestine and Israel.

Chapter 9

Iraq's Troubles and Its Effect on the Gaza Crisis

Iraq's troubled history and ongoing struggles have had a profound and multifaceted impact on the Gaza crisis. The country's challenges extend beyond sectarian divisions, political instability, external interventions, security concerns, and socioeconomic issues, significantly hampering its ability to effectively address the Israeli-Palestinian conflict.

Iraq's sectarian divisions have deep historical roots that continue to shape the country's dynamics. The Shia-Sunni divide dates back centuries, intertwined with religious, political, and societal tensions. After the fall of Saddam Hussein in 2003, Iraq experienced a power vacuum, leading to a rise in sectarian violence and further deterioration of communal relations. To exacerbate matters, the issue of Kurdish autonomy in the northern region also adds another layer of complexity to Iraq's internal divisions. The sensitive balance and interaction between these different sectarian and ethnic groups make it exceedingly difficult for Iraq to forge a unified position on the Gaza crisis.

Political instability is another significant hindrance to Iraq's engagement in the Gaza crisis. The country has intricately struggled to establish stable governance since the ousting of Saddam Hussein. Frequent changes in leadership, weak institutions, and deep-seated corruption have prevented Iraq from developing a coherent approach towards the Israeli-Palestinian conflict. The volatile political landscape has perpetuated a culture of in-fighting, rivalries, and lack of consensus among various political factions, diverting attention away from external affairs. As a result, Iraq's ability to effectively advocate for the Palestinians or contribute substantively to resolving the Gaza crisis has been severely compromised.

External interventions have played a consequential role in Iraq and have further complicated its involvement in the Gaza crisis. Neighbouring regional powers, such as Iran and Saudi Arabia, have used Iraq as a proxy battleground to exert their influence and pursue their own geopolitical interests. These external actors often support divergent factions within Iraq, exacerbating the country's fragmentation and impeding its ability to present a unified front on regional issues. The competing agendas of these external powers continue to cast a shadow over Iraq's capacity to play a constructive role in resolving the Israeli-Palestinian conflict.

Iraq's security challenges pose a formidable obstacle to meaningful engagement in the Gaza crisis. The country's struggle against various extremist groups, including the Islamic State (ISIS), has demanded significant resources and military efforts. The fight against terrorism has absorbed a substantial portion of Iraq's attention, leaving limited room for active participation in resolving conflicts beyond its borders. The imperative to stabilise the country, protect its citizens, and prevent the resurgence of extremist groups has inevitably taken precedence over external matters like the Gaza crisis.

Furthermore, Iraq's socioeconomic issues have further constrained its involvement in the Gaza crisis. Rampant corruption, high unemployment rates, inadequate public services, and economic disparities have fuelled public discontent and protests throughout the country. These internal challenges have diverted resources, attention, and energy from external conflicts. Addressing the pressing needs of the population and alleviating socioeconomic grievances have become urgent priorities for the Iraqi government, leaving fewer resources available to actively engage in international crises like the Israeli-Palestinian conflict.

In conclusion, the deep-rooted and complex troubles faced by Iraq continue to impede its ability to effectively address the Gaza crisis. Sectarian divisions, political instability, external interventions, security concerns, and socioeconomic issues have all contributed to Iraq's limited capacity to play a significant role in the Israeli-Palestinian conflict. Overcoming these challenges necessitates concerted efforts to bridge communal divides, establish stable governance, minimise external interference, strengthen security, and address socioeconomic disparities. Only then can Iraq allocate the necessary resources, attention, and engagement to contribute meaningfully to the resolution of the Gaza crisis and support the aspirations of the Palestinian people.

Chapter 10

Jordan's Pressures and its Attempt to Mediate

Jordan, a key player in the Middle East, has often found itself at the forefront of efforts to mediate between Israel and Palestine. This chapter delves into the historical, political, and geographical context of Jordan, shedding light on the pressures it faces in attempting to navigate the complexities of the Israeli-Palestinian conflict.

Geographically, Jordan is intricately intertwined with the conflict, sharing borders with both Israel and Palestine. This proximity places Jordan at the forefront of any regional unrest or escalations, making it acutely aware of the implications of the conflict on its own security and stability. The potential for spillover effects and the influx of refugees into Jordan further exacerbate the challenges it faces in maintaining peace and stability within its own borders.

Furthermore, Jordan's unique historical and political context adds complexity to its mediation efforts. This Hashemite Kingdom has a peace treaty with Israel, signed in 1994, which marked a significant milestone in the region. The treaty established diplomatic relations and fostered economic ties between the two countries. Over the years, Jordan has benefited from this relationship, with increased trade, tourism, and regional cooperation. However, the peace treaty has not been without its critics within Jordan, who argue that Israel continues to violate Palestinian rights, leading to ongoing scepticism and discontent.

On the other hand, Jordan maintains a close affinity and common Arab identity with the Palestinians. It has a considerable population of Palestinian refugees, who have sought shelter and livelihoods within its borders. This historical connection and shared experience shape Jordan's stance on the conflict. With a deep sense of solidarity, Jordan stands in support of the Palestinian struggle for self-determination and a just resolution to the conflict.

The duality of Jordan's relationships, both with Israel and Palestine, highlights the delicate balancing act it must perform in its mediation efforts. While it seeks to maintain stable relations with its neighbour Israel and safeguard its own security, Jordan also has a moral and political responsibility to support the Palestinian cause and work towards a just resolution.

Under the leadership of King Abdullah II, Jordan has played a significant role in facilitating peace talks and dialogue between Israel and Palestine. The king himself has been actively involved in various peace initiatives and has consistently advocated for a two-state solution. Recognising the importance of a comprehensive approach, Jordan has hosted numerous high-level meetings, negotiations, and summits, providing a neutral ground for the parties involved.

Jordan has put forth several peace proposals and initiatives throughout its history of mediation. One significant effort was the Arab Peace Initiative in 2002, which was endorsed by the Arab League. This initiative called for Israel's complete withdrawal from the occupied territories in exchange for normalising relations with the Arab states. The Arab Peace Initiative aimed to achieve a comprehensive, just, and lasting resolution to the conflict, addressing the core issues of borders, refugees, and Jerusalem.

In addition to its independent initiatives, Jordan has actively engaged in international endeavours to promote peace in the region. It has been part of the Quartet on the Middle East, along with the United Nations, the United States, and the European Union, which works to facilitate peace negotiations between Israel and Palestine. Jordan has also participated in the Paris Peace Conference and supported the United Nations' efforts to find a peaceful resolution.

However, mediating between Israel and Palestine is not without its challenges. Jordan encounters internal divisions within the Palestinian leadership and the fragmentation of Palestinian territories, which undermine the effectiveness of its mediation efforts. The division between Fatah and Hamas has hampered progress, making it difficult for Jordan to engage with a united and representative Palestinian authority.

External pressures from other Arab states further complicate Jordan's mediation attempts, as each state pursues its own interests and considerations regarding the Israeli-Palestinian conflict. These regional dynamics and differing positions often impose additional hurdles, impeding progress towards a resolution.

The influence of international actors, particularly the United States, cannot be overlooked in Jordan's mediation efforts. Historically, the United States has played a significant role as a mediator in the Israeli-Palestinian conflict. Jordan navigates expectations and pressures from the United States while also considering its own national interests. Balancing these external influences with its regional responsibilities requires careful diplomacy and strategic decision-making.

Despite these multifaceted challenges, Jordan remains committed to its role as a mediator and advocate for peace in the region. It strives to mobilise international support for the two-state solution and consistently emphasises the urgency of finding a just resolution based on international law and United Nations resolutions. Jordan's diplomatic efforts extend beyond mediating between Israel and Palestine, as it actively engages with various international forums to promote a peaceful resolution and highlight the devastating consequences of further delays.

In conclusion, Jordan's historical ties, geographical proximity, and strategic interests make it an essential player in mediating the Israeli-Palestinian conflict. The pressures it faces from internal, regional, and international dynamics are significant but not insurmountable. Jordan's unwavering commitment to regional stability and the pursuit of a just and lasting peace drive its mediation efforts. As it navigates the complex web of competing interests, Jordan plays a crucial role in fostering dialogue, negotiations, and international support for a peaceful resolution to the conflict.

Chapter 11

Kuwait's Challenges in Supporting Palestine

Kuwait, a small but influential Arab state, has faced its fair share of challenges in supporting the Palestinian cause. While the government of Kuwait has historically shown solidarity with Palestine and has made efforts to provide financial aid, there are various impediments that hinder its ability to fully support the Palestinian struggle for statehood.

One of the major challenges Kuwait faces is its delicate geopolitical position. Situated in a region characterised by political instability and ongoing conflicts, Kuwait must carefully navigate its relationships with neighbouring countries, particularly those that have normalised relations with Israel. This often puts Kuwait in a difficult position, as they must balance their commitment to supporting Palestine with the need to maintain regional stability and diplomatic relations.

The normalisation of relations between some Arab states and Israel has added complexity to Kuwait's support for Palestine. The Abraham Accords, signed in 2020, saw the United Arab Emirates, Bahrain, Sudan, and Morocco establish diplomatic ties with Israel. This development has created divisions within the Arab world, with some countries arguing for engagement with Israel as a means to influence its policies towards Palestine, while others like Kuwait maintain that normalisation should only occur after a meaningful resolution to the conflict is achieved. Kuwait, with its historical commitment to Palestinian rights, finds itself on the side of advocating for Palestinian rights and is hesitant about aligning itself with moves towards normalisation.

A key factor in Kuwait's geopolitical challenges is the Gulf Cooperation Council (GCC), a regional alliance consisting of Bahrain, Kuwait, Oman, Qatar, Saudi Arabia, and the United Arab Emirates (UAE). While each member state has its own stance on supporting Palestine, the GCC as a collective entity has refrained from taking strong, unified actions against Israel. This discord within the GCC can limit Kuwait's ability to pursue bold measures in support of Palestine, as it must consider the consequences of diverging from the consensus within the alliance.

Moreover, Kuwait faces internal challenges in its support for Palestine. While the majority of Kuwaiti citizens express solidarity with the Palestinian cause, there are also dissenting voices within the population. These dissenting voices often argue that Kuwait should prioritise its own national interests and focus on domestic issues rather than funnelling resources towards Palestine. This internal divide complicates Kuwait's ability to act decisively in supporting the Palestinian struggle and creates a balancing act for the government in appeasing public sentiment.

Economic considerations also play a significant role in Kuwait's challenges in supporting Palestine. As an oil-dependant economy, Kuwait must carefully manage its financial resources and prioritise its own national development. While Kuwait has historically been generous in providing financial aid to Palestine, there are limitations to the amount of assistance it can offer. Fluctuations in oil prices and economic uncertainties can strain Kuwait's ability to maintain a consistent level of support for the Palestinian cause. Furthermore, Kuwait faces the challenge of allocating a portion of its budget towards Palestine without compromising its own economic stability and welfare programmes for its citizens.

Furthermore, Kuwait faces geopolitical pressures from larger powers that can influence its stance on supporting Palestine. These pressures come from both regional and international players, who may have their own agendas and strategic calculations. The Israeli-Palestinian conflict is a complex issue intertwined with various regional dynamics, and Kuwait must navigate its relationships with influential powers such as the United States, European Union, and other Arab states. These powers hold significant sway over Kuwait's decisions and can exert pressure on Kuwait to align its policies with their interests, potentially hindering full-fledged support for Palestine.

Additionally, Kuwait faces challenges related to the effectiveness of its aid efforts. While Kuwait has provided substantial financial assistance to Palestine, the impact of this aid on the ground is often limited due to various factors. Administrative inefficiencies, corruption within the Palestinian Authority, and the ongoing Israeli occupation can impede the successful implementation of Kuwaiti aid projects. Kuwait must address these critical issues to ensure that its support effectively contributes to sustainable development and the improvement of living conditions for Palestinians.

Furthermore, Kuwait's support for Palestine also extends to diplomatic efforts. The country actively participates in international conferences, such as the United Nations General Assembly and the Arab League, where it advocates for a just and lasting solution to the Israeli-Palestinian conflict. Kuwait consistently emphasises the need for a two-state solution, an end to Israeli settlement expansion, and the recognition of East Jerusalem as the capital of a future Palestinian state. Through diplomatic channels, Kuwait aims to raise awareness about the plight of the Palestinian people and garner international support for their aspirations.

Despite these challenges, Kuwait continues to play a role in supporting Palestine through diplomatic channels, humanitarian aid, and advocacy for Palestinian rights on international platforms. Kuwait understands the urgency of the Palestinian struggle for self-determination and recognises the need to address the political, economic, and humanitarian dimensions of the conflict. While navigating its limitations, Kuwait remains committed to utilising its resources, influence, and diplomatic channels to support Palestine. The country envisions a just and lasting resolution to the Israeli-Palestinian conflict, where Palestinians can exercise their rights, live in dignity, and establish an independent state. By persevering in its efforts, Kuwait stands with the Palestinian people in their pursuit of justice and a brighter future.

Chapter 12

Lebanon's Position and the Internal Issues that Hamper Resolution

Lebanon, a small nation nestled in the heart of the Middle East, finds itself entangled in the complexities of the Israeli-Palestinian conflict. This position stems not only from its geographical proximity but also from a historical connection to the Palestinian cause. However, the nation is beset by a multitude of internal issues, deeply rooted and intricate, that significantly hinder its ability to effectively contribute to the resolution efforts.

One of the main challenges Lebanon faces is the presence and control of powerful non-state actors within its territory. Hezbollah, a Lebanese Shia political and military organisation, wields considerable influence over the country. Originally established in the early 1980s as a resistance movement against the Israeli occupation of southern Lebanon, Hezbollah has transformed into a formidable force that plays a pivotal role in Lebanese politics. It operates an extensive social welfare network, providing essential services to its constituents, which has solidified its popularity among certain segments of the population. However, this influence has also provoked controversy and criticism, as some view Hezbollah's actions, such as its active military involvement in the Syrian civil war and its conflict with Israel, as exacerbating tensions and undermining the prospects for peace in the region.

The political landscape in Lebanon is intricately fragmented, with diverse factions representing various religious and sectarian communities. This fragmentation is a direct result of Lebanon's unique power-sharing system, known as confessionalism. With confessionalism, the aim is to maintain a delicate balance among the different religious groups in the country. While this system may ostensibly promote inclusivity, it often results in political paralysis, making it arduous for the country to form a unified position on the Israeli-Palestinian conflict. The intricate web of alliances and rivalries among the Lebanese political elite further complicates efforts to present a coherent stance, particularly when addressing crucial issues like disarmament and the integration of Hezbollah into the political mainstream.

In addition to these internal challenges, Lebanon grapples with its own security concerns and historical grievances. The country has a long and turbulent history with Israel, marked by conflicts such as the 1982 Israeli invasion and the subsequent occupation of southern Lebanon lasting until 2000. Memories of these tumultuous times and the ongoing security threats near the border shape Lebanon's approach to the Israeli-Palestinian conflict, often fuelling a deep-seated sense of mistrust towards Israeli actions and policies. The volatile situation along the Blue Line, the dae facto border between Israel and Lebanon, continues to pose potential risks and trigger escalations that divert attention from broader efforts to resolve the Israeli-Palestinian conflict.

Lebanon's complex relationship with its neighbouring country, Syria, also plays a significant role in its approach to the conflict. The Syrian civil war, which erupted in 2011, has had profound implications for Lebanon. The conflict spilt over into Lebanese territory, intensifying existing tensions and exacerbating sectarian divisions within the country. Various Lebanese factions aligned themselves with either the Syrian government or the opposition, further fragmenting an already divided political landscape. This intricate web of allegiances and competing interests makes it increasingly challenging for Lebanon to form a united front regarding the Israeli-Palestinian conflict, as the internal schisms created by the Syrian conflict compound existing challenges.

Furthermore, Lebanon's socioeconomic challenges and the persistent influx of Palestinian refugees continue to strain the nation's resources and complicate its involvement in the Israeli-Palestinian conflict. Lebanon has been hosting Palestinian refugees since the mass displacement that occurred during the 1948 Arab-Israeli war and subsequent conflicts. Palestinian refugee camps, such as Shatila and Ain al-Hilweh, have become permanent fixtures within the country, housing generations of displaced Palestinians. However, the integration of these refugees into Lebanese society remains a contentious issue, with some arguing that the camps perpetuate a sense of displacement and hinder the country's ability to focus on external conflicts. The socioeconomic strain on Lebanon's infrastructure, economy, and social fabric resulting from this protracted refugee crisis further exacerbates existing tensions and complicates any meaningful engagement in resolving the Israeli-Palestinian conflict.

Overcoming these internal obstacles is of paramount importance for Lebanon to play a more constructive role in promoting peace, stability, and lasting resolution in the region. The presence of powerful non-state actors, political fragmentation, security concerns, historical grievances, and socioeconomic challenges all contribute to the complexity of Lebanon's approach to the Israeli-Palestinian conflict. By addressing these internal issues, Lebanon can enhance its position as a potential facilitator and bring much-needed stability to a region yearning for a just and lasting peace.

Chapter 13

Libya's Role and Its Struggles to Influence the Conflict

L ibya has historically played a significant role in the Israeli-Palestinian conflict, standing firmly in support of the Palestinian cause. However, its ability to actively shape the conflict has been marred by the internal struggles and political instability that have plagued the country since the downfall of Muammar Gaddafi's regime in 2011.

Under Gaddafi's rule, Libya emerged as a forceful advocate for the Palestinian Liberation Organisation (PLO) and its leader, Yasser Arafat. Gaddafi, driven by anti-Israel sentiments, provided substantial financial aid and firearms to the Palestinian cause, positioning Libya as a sanctuary for PLO operatives and passionate supporters. Libya's backing extended beyond rhetoric, as it allowed the PLO to establish offices in the capital city of Tripoli and supplied the Palestinian fighters with arms through clandestine channels. In fact, it was in Libya where the PLO famously declared an independent Palestinian state in 1988.

Gaddafi's charismatic personality and pan-Arabist ideology attracted other Arab states to join Libya's stance against Israel. This led to the formation of the Arab Deterrent Force, a coalition of North African and Middle Eastern countries, which aimed to counter Israel's military might. Through funding, training, and coordination, Libya played a pivotal role in bolstering the capabilities of Palestinian militants, initially helping them fight against Israeli forces during the early years of the conflict.

However, after the Arab Spring uprisings and Gaddafi's overthrow, Libya witnessed the disintegration of centralised authority, giving way to political fragmentation and armed conflicts. Competing factions emerged, each vying for power, and the aspirations for a democratic transition took a tumultuous path. This internal chaos disoriented Libya, diverting its attention and resources away from regional conflicts, including the Israeli-Palestinian issue.

The political instability that ensued hampered Libya's capacity to exert influence on the Israeli-Palestinian conflict in a cohesive manner. As the country struggled to establish a unified government, different factions and armed groups proliferated, each with its own objectives and ideologies. Some aligned themselves with Islamist movements or militias, while others focused on local control and autonomy. These divisions further complicated Libya's stance on the Israeli-Palestinian issue, thwarting its ability to project a consolidated and consistent position.

Consequently, Libya's role in shaping the Israeli-Palestinian conflict became weakened, with the country's efforts to advocate for the Palestinian cause constantly undermined by internal divisions. The absence of a stable government hindered Libya's ability to engage effectively with international actors and Arab states, as it lacked the necessary political authority to make impactful contributions to the conflict's resolution.

Moreover, regional powers have seized the opportunity presented by Libya's vulnerabilities to assert their own interests in the Israeli-Palestinian conflict. Countries such as Egypt, Saudi Arabia, and the United Arab Emirates, pursuing their own geopolitical goals, supported rival factions in Libya, further exacerbating the country's internal conflicts and diminishing its influence on the Israeli-Palestinian issue.

To regain its position as a significant player in the region and effectively influence the Israeli-Palestinian conflict, Libya must address its internal divisions and establish a stable governance structure. Such a government would be capable of effectively engaging with international actors, neighbouring Arab states, and regional organisations to advocate for the rights of the Palestinian people. Only through unity and stability can Libya reclaim its historical role and effectively contribute to the resolution of the Israeli-Palestinian conflict, bringing about a lasting peace in the region.

It is worthwhile to note that Libya's current situation does not solely define its historical contributions to the Israeli-Palestinian conflict. The country's prominent role in the past, its support for the Palestinian cause, and its influence within certain Arab circles cannot be disregarded. While the present struggles overshadow Libya's potential impact, there remains hope that with perseverance and a concerted effort to resolve internal conflicts, Libya can restore its role as a key player in shaping the Israeli-Palestinian conflict. The resolution of Libya's challenges depends on the collective will of its people, aspiring for a stable and unified government that can effectively channel Libya's historical commitment into meaningful actions for the benefit of the Palestinian people.

Chapter 14

Mauritania's Dilemma and Its Impact on the Palestinian Struggle

D espite its relatively small size and influence on the global stage, Mauritania's stance on the conflict carries significance due to its geographical location and historical ties with Arab states. We will explore in greater detail the complexities of Mauritania's position and the impact it has on the Palestinian struggle for statehood.

Mauritania, located in Northwest Africa, shares borders with Algeria, Senegal, Mali, and Western Sahara. Historically, Mauritania has maintained close ties with Arab states, aligning itself with the Arab League and staunchly supporting the Palestinian cause. However, the country has faced internal challenges and external pressures that have shaped its approach to the Israeli-Palestinian conflict.

One major factor influencing Mauritania's stance is its internal political dynamics. Since gaining independence from France in 1960, Mauritania has witnessed multiple coup d'états and changes in leadership, leading to shifting foreign policies. These transitions have often impacted Mauritania's approach to the Israeli-Palestinian conflict. Notably, in 1999, a peaceful transfer of power occurred, bringing President Maaouiya Ould Sid'Ahmed Taya to office, shifting the country's stance towards a more moderate and dialogue-based approach to the conflict. However, subsequent political instability, including a coup in 2005, led by Colonel Ely Ould Mohamed Vall, followed by democratic elections in 2007, led to uncertainties in Mauritania's foreign policy positions. We will delve into the impact of these internal dynamics on Mauritania's ability to effectively support Palestine and contribute to the resolution of the conflict.

External influences also play a crucial role in shaping Mauritania's stance. As a member of the Arab League, Mauritania aligns itself with the collective position of Arab states regarding the Israeli-Palestinian conflict. However, differences within the Arab world present challenges for Mauritania's unequivocal support for Palestine. Countries like Egypt and Jordan, which have signed peace treaties with Israel, advocate for a negotiated solution and a two-state solution, while others like Syria and Lebanon lean towards a more confrontational approach. Mauritania finds itself navigating these complex dynamics while trying to maintain its commitment to the Palestinian struggle.

Furthermore, Mauritania's geographical proximity to Western Sahara introduces additional complexities. The Western Sahara conflict divides Arab states, as some recognise and support the Polisario Front's quest for independence, while others, including Mauritania, maintain diplomatic relations with Morocco, which claims sovereignty over the region. Balancing these relationships requires Mauritania to tread cautiously, as its position on the Western Sahara dispute could potentially impact its ability to advocate strongly for the Palestinian cause.

Another significant aspect we will examine in greater detail is Mauritania's socio-economic challenges and their impact on its involvement in the conflict. Despite its vast resources such as iron ore, gold, and oil, Mauritania faces internal economic hurdles such as poverty, unemployment, and resource scarcity. These pressing concerns often divert its attention away from international issues, limiting its capacity to fully engage in the Palestinian struggle. Limited economic resources and the urgent need for development may hinder Mauritania from making substantive contributions to addressing the conflict's core issues. We will explore the specific socio-economic factors and their implications on Mauritania's ability to actively support Palestine.

Additionally, Mauritania's engagement with regional and international organisations plays a vital role in its involvement in the conflict. As a member of the Arab League and the African Union, Mauritania actively participates in diplomatic initiatives aimed at resolving the Israeli-Palestinian conflict. Its involvement in peace initiatives led by entities such as the United Nations and the Arab League can shape its relationship with Palestine and Israel. We will assess the effectiveness of these organizations' efforts in mobilising support for Palestine within Mauritania and the wider Arab world, examining specific initiatives and their outcomes.

Moreover, Mauritania's position on the Israeli-Palestinian conflict is also influenced by its historical ties with Palestine. Over the years, Mauritania has developed cultural, political, and economic connections with the Palestinians, which have contributed to its empathetic stance. The Palestinian Liberation Organisation (PLO) has long enjoyed support from Mauritania, and many Palestinians have sought refuge in the country. Understanding these historical ties provides critical context to Mauritania's actions and positions in relation to the Israeli-Palestinian conflict.

In conclusion, this extended chapter expands on the complexities of Mauritania's dilemma in navigating the Israeli-Palestinian conflict and the impact it has on the Palestinian struggle. By further exploring Mauritania's internal political dynamics, external pressures, socio-economic challenges, historical ties with Palestine, and engagement with regional and international organisations, we gain a more comprehensive understanding of its positioning on the conflict and its ability to effectively support the Palestinian cause. Understanding these multifaceted aspects sheds light on the broader dynamics of the conflict and highlights the significance of smaller nations in influencing its resolution.

Chapter 15

Morocco's Stance and the Factors That Hinder Progress

Morocco, a North African country with a rich historical and cultural heritage, has long been involved in the Israeli-Palestinian conflict, seeking to contribute to peace initiatives and support Palestine's pursuit of statehood. However, this commitment has been hindered by various complex factors that have impacted Morocco's ability to address the conflict effectively and work towards a resolution.

One of the significant factors that have impeded progress for Morocco is its intricate relationship with Israel. Morocco and Israel maintain diplomatic and economic ties, and Morocco is among the few Arab countries that have openly engaged in direct relations with Israel. This relationship has deep roots in the historical connections between Morocco's Jewish community and the state of Israel. Morocco's Jewish community, one of the largest in the Arab world, has played a crucial role in shaping the perceptions of the Israeli-Palestinian conflict within Morocco. The close ties between Morocco and its Jewish community, combined with historical and cultural factors, have created a delicate balancing act for the Moroccan government as it seeks to maintain positive relations with both Israel and the Arab world.

This delicate balancing act has, at times, compromised Morocco's stance on the conflict and weakened its position as an impartial mediator. Arab states and Palestinian leadership have expressed concerns about Morocco's engagement with Israel, viewing it as a form of normalisation. Credibility has been lost among certain factions within the Palestinian community and other Arab countries, making it challenging for Morocco to exercise significant influence in the peace process. Despite these challenges, Morocco continues to emphasise its commitment to Palestinian statehood and its belief in a two-state solution.

Morocco's internal challenges also hinder its progress in addressing the Israeli-Palestinian conflict. The Western Sahara conflict, a longstanding territorial dispute between Morocco and the Polisario Front seeking independence, diverts Morocco's attention and resources away from actively engaging in mediating the Israeli-Palestinian conflict. This internal issue has limited Morocco's capacity to devote substantial political capital and resources to play a more significant role in resolving the Israeli-Palestinian conflict. However, Morocco acknowledges that the resolution of the Israeli-Palestinian conflict could have positive implications for other regional conflicts, including the Western Sahara issue, and remains committed to exploring opportunities for peace.

Another factor hindering Morocco's progress is the lack of unity within the Arab world regarding strategies towards the Israeli-Palestinian conflict. Arab states have differing priorities and interests, making it challenging for Morocco to form a cohesive Arab stance. Disagreements among Arab countries regarding the recognition of Israel, settlement policies, and negotiation strategies weaken Morocco's position and limit the possibilities for collective action and effective diplomacy.

Moreover, external influences and geopolitical considerations also have a significant impact on Morocco's approach to the Israeli-Palestinian conflict. Global powers, such as the United States and the European Union, often exert their influence in the region to protect their own interests. These external actors have their own policies and agendas, which can complicate Morocco's efforts to assert its own position in the conflict and pursue effective diplomacy. The involvement of global powers can sometimes overshadow Morocco's initiative and limit its ability to act as an independent actor in mediating and resolving the conflict.

Despite these hurdles, Morocco has shown resilience and remains committed to supporting Palestine's aspirations for statehood. The country understands the importance of a just and lasting solution to the Israeli-Palestinian conflict for regional stability and prosperity. Morocco continues to explore avenues for peace, engage in diplomatic efforts, and foster dialogue to contribute to a resolution. As it navigates the intricate web of internal and external challenges, Morocco holds onto the belief that a comprehensive and fair resolution to the conflict is necessary for a collective and prosperous future in the region.

Chapter 16

Oman's Position and the Challenges It Faces in Gaza

O man, a small nation situated on the eastern edge of the Arabian Peninsula, has long maintained a reputation for its unwavering commitment to neutrality and diplomacy in the Middle East. In this extended chapter, we delve deeper into Oman's position and the substantial challenges it faces in the ongoing Israeli-Palestinian conflict, specifically in the context of the Gaza situation.

Oman's historical approach to the Israeli-Palestinian conflict has been steadfastly rooted in a commitment to peace, stability, and the promotion of dialogue. Throughout the years, the country has advocated for a peaceful resolution through negotiations, firmly believing that a comprehensive and just solution is essential for long-term peace in the region. Oman has consistently emphasised the importance of recognising the rights of the Palestinian people, including the establishment of an independent state with East Jerusalem as its capital, based on the borders prior to the 1967 war.

However, Oman's involvement in the Gaza situation presents several complex challenges. Chief among them is the limited influence they possess over the parties involved. While Oman is respected for its diplomatic efforts, it lacks the same level of political or economic leverage as some of its larger regional counterparts. As a result, their ability to actively contribute to resolving the conflict may be constrained, as their influence may be overshadowed by more prominent and influential powers. Nevertheless, Oman's steadfast commitment to neutrality and fostering dialogue provides a valuable platform for facilitating negotiations and promoting constructive engagement between the Israeli and Palestinian sides.

Considering Oman's geographic location, the nation faces unique challenges in its engagement with the Gaza situation. Situated on the southeastern coast of the Arabian Peninsula, Oman shares borders with Saudi Arabia, the United Arab Emirates, and Yemen. Its proximity to the Strait of Hormuz, a vital shipping route for oil exports, also adds an additional layer of complexity. Oman must navigate carefully to maintain neutral ground, ensuring that none of its actions are misconstrued as favouring one side over the other. Oman fully recognises the importance of collective security for the region but also acknowledges the necessity of addressing the legitimate grievances and aspirations of the Palestinian people.

Furthermore, Oman encounters the challenge of striking a delicate balance between their commitment to non-interference and their desire to support the rights of the Palestinian people. The country has consistently expressed solidarity with the Palestinian cause and has provided humanitarian aid to the Gaza Strip. However, with limited resources, Oman's efforts may not be sufficient to meet the deep-rooted humanitarian and socio-economic challenges faced by the people of Gaza. Seeking to alleviate this, Oman has actively sought to support international efforts in providing humanitarian assistance and has repeatedly called for collective action to ensure the well-being and long-term prosperity of the Palestinian population.

Internally, Oman faces its own unique dynamics and challenges. The country's political structure is an absolute monarchy, with Sultan Qaboos bin Said Al Said at the helm. Under his rule, Oman has maintained stability for several decades. However, concerns over succession and potential internal power struggles may ultimately impact Oman's ability to maintain its neutral stance and actively engage in the resolution of the Israeli-Palestinian conflict. Oman's leadership transition, whenever it occurs, will undoubtedly have significant implications for the country's foreign policy, including its stance on the Israeli-Palestinian conflict.

In conclusion, Oman's position within the Israeli-Palestinian conflict, specifically concerning the Gaza situation, is characterised by its unwavering commitment to neutrality, diplomacy, and the promotion of dialogue. Despite the substantial challenges it faces, Oman remains determined in its pursuit of a peaceful resolution and in addressing the pressing humanitarian needs of the Palestinian people. Whilst its influence and resources may be limited when compared to larger regional powers, Oman's consistent efforts serve as a powerful reminder that even smaller nations can play a meaningful role in facilitating peace and stability in the Israeli-Palestinian conflict.

Chapter 17

Palestine's Struggle for Statehood and Its Interactions with Arab States

The quest for statehood has been a constant and arduous struggle for Palestine throughout the Israeli-Palestinian conflict. This chapter delves deeper into the historical background of Palestine's pursuit of statehood and explores its interactions with Arab states in greater detail, shedding light on the complexities, challenges, and nuances faced in the process.

The struggle for Palestinian statehood can be traced back to the early 20th century when the Zionist movement gathered momentum, propelled by the ideals of Jewish self-determination. The Balfour Declaration of 1917 marked a pivotal moment in this narrative, as the British government expressed support for the establishment of a "national home for the Jewish people" in Palestine. However, the declaration did not adequately consider the rights and aspirations of the indigenous Palestinian population, setting the stage for decades of tension, conflict, and displacement.

As the Zionist movement gained traction, Arab states in the region grew increasingly concerned about the potential marginalisation and displacement of Palestinians from their ancestral lands. The Arab world's support for Palestine's statehood took shape as a reaction to this perceived threat, with the overarching goal of safeguarding the rights, welfare, and aspirations of Palestinians. Throughout the turbulent course of history, the status of Palestine has become intrinsically linked to the Arab identity and the broader Arab-Israeli conflict.

Over the years, Palestinian leaders sought support from their Arab brethren to advance their cause. The Arab League, an organisation composed of Arab nations, assumed a central role in advocating for Palestinian rights on the international stage. Arab states provided financial aid, diplomatic support, and military assistance to Palestine in its struggle for self-determination. These states recognised the shared Arab identity and historical, cultural, and religious ties that bound them to the Palestinian cause, amplifying their commitment to Palestinian statehood.

However, the solidarity among Arab states regarding Palestine has not always been unwavering. Internal divisions, differing national interests, and regional power dynamics have, at times, hampered collective action. While they shared a common concern for Palestinian rights and aspirations, Arab states differed in their approach to the Israeli-Palestinian conflict, with some prioritising their own national interests over Palestinian statehood.

In the wake of the 1967 Six-Day War, in which Israel occupied the West Bank, including East Jerusalem, and the Gaza Strip, Arab states united in their support for Palestine by passing the "Three No's" resolution: no peace with Israel, no recognition of Israel, and no negotiation with Israel. The resolution represented a powerful display of unity and determination to seek justice for Palestinians.

The Oslo Accords, signed in the 1990s, represented a significant turning point in Palestine's struggle for statehood. These accords aimed to create a framework for peace negotiations between Israel and Palestine, facilitated by international actors. Arab states, including Egypt and Jordan, played a crucial role in supporting the peace process and encouraging diplomatic relations between the two sides.

Nevertheless, despite international efforts and Arab support, the path to Palestinian statehood has been fraught with obstacles. The continued Israeli occupation of Palestinian territories, the expansion of settlements, and the lack of progress in negotiations have severely hindered the realisation of an independent Palestinian state. Arab states have voiced their frustration with the lack of tangible progress and have faced limitations in their ability to influence the situation due to the geopolitical realities and shifting international dynamics.

In recent years, the Palestinian struggle for statehood has faced further challenges. Political divisions between Fatah and Hamas, governance issues, and the changing geopolitical landscape in the region have added complexities to the quest for statehood. Arab states have had to navigate these challenges while continuing to support the Palestinian cause, their efforts often fragmented due to differing national priorities, strategic considerations, and domestic political dynamics.

The pursuit of statehood for Palestine remains a contentious, complex, and difficult process, deeply rooted in historical, political, and humanitarian issues. The interactions between Palestine and Arab states have shaped the dynamics of the Israeli-Palestinian conflict, exposing the intricate web of historical, political, and regional complexities that impede the achievement of a just and lasting resolution. The road to Palestinian statehood continues to be ardently pursued amidst ongoing challenges, necessitating sustained international support and a concerted effort to address the multifaceted issues at play.

Chapter 18

Qatar's Role in the Gaza War and Its Efforts for Peace

Q atar, a small but influential country in the Middle East, has played a significant and multifaceted role in the Israeli-Palestinian conflict, particularly during the Gaza War. Despite its size, Qatar has been able to exert its influence through diplomatic channels, financial support, and its strategic positioning, making it a key mediator in the conflict.

During the Gaza War, Qatar took a proactive and engaged approach in seeking a resolution. Recognising the urgency of the situation in Gaza and the devastating impact the conflict was having on the Palestinian population, Qatar's leadership mobilised its resources and networks to facilitate dialogue and encourage negotiations between the conflicting parties. Through its diplomatic channels, Qatar engaged actively with both Israeli and Palestinian leaders, as well as regional and international actors, to emphasise the importance of finding a peaceful solution while acknowledging the complexity and sensitivities of the conflict.

One of the notable achievements of Qatar during the Gaza War was its instrumental role in brokering a ceasefire between Israel and Hamas. Qatar utilised its extensive diplomatic network and relationships with key stakeholders to facilitate constructive dialogue and encourage both parties to consider a cessation of hostilities. This mediation effort showcased Qatar's commitment to peace and its ability to bridge gaps between conflicting parties. By leveraging its relationships with various international actors, including the United Nations, the Arab League, and regional stakeholders, Qatar effectively paved the way for constructive negotiations and ultimately a ceasefire agreement.

It's vital to note that Qatar's engagement with Hamas, the governing authority in Gaza, has been met with some criticism and controversy from certain international actors who view the group as a terrorist organisation. However, Qatar has defended its engagement with Hamas, arguing that it is necessary to engage with all relevant parties in order to achieve lasting peace. Qatar, along with other regional actors, has supported the notion that excluding Hamas from the peace process could hinder progress and potentially lead to further violence and unrest.

In addition to its mediation efforts, Qatar has been an active and vocal participant in regional and international forums aimed at addressing the Israeli-Palestinian conflict. The country has utilised its membership in the United Nations and the Arab League to advocate for the rights of Palestinians and draw attention to the humanitarian crisis in Gaza. Qatar has consistently called for an end to the Israeli blockade on Gaza, emphasising the need for the free movement of goods and people to alleviate the socio-economic challenges faced by the region. Through its active participation in these forums, Qatar has sought to ensure that the voices of the Palestinians are heard and their rights are upheld within the international community.

Moreover, Qatar's commitment to peace extended beyond diplomatic efforts. Recognising the devastating impact of the conflict on the infrastructure and livelihoods of the Palestinian people, Qatar pledged significant financial aid to support the reconstruction and development of Gaza following the war. This commitment encompassed rebuilding damaged infrastructure, hospitals, schools, and housing in the region. Qatar's substantial financial aid not only demonstrated its commitment to peace but also served as a tangible gesture to alleviate the suffering of the Palestinian population. The country's support for rebuilding efforts aimed to enhance the prospects for stability and prosperity in the region.

In conclusion, Qatar has played a pivotal and multi-dimensional role in the Israeli-Palestinian conflict and the Gaza War. Through its diplomatic engagement, mediation efforts, active participation in international forums, and significant financial support, Qatar has demonstrated a genuine commitment to finding a just and lasting solution for the conflict. While Qatar's involvement, particularly its engagement with Hamas, has faced criticism, its efforts have been aimed at fostering dialogue, bridging gaps, and advancing the cause of peace. As the conflict continues to evolve, Qatar's role is likely to remain significant, as it strives to find a long-term, just, and sustainable resolution for the Israeli-Palestinian conflict.

Chapter 19

Saudi Arabia's Complex Position and the Factors That Limit Its Influence

S audi Arabia's role in the Israeli-Palestinian conflict is highly complex, influenced by a myriad of factors that both enable and limit its ability to exert influence on the situation. As one of the most prominent Arab states and a significant regional power, Saudi Arabia faces a delicate balancing act in navigating its position in the conflict.

Historically, Saudi Arabia has supported Palestinian statehood and advocated for the rights of the Palestinian people. The kingdom, being the birthplace of Islam, has a significant moral responsibility to defend Muslim interests worldwide, including the just Palestinian cause. Saudi Arabia has also been an advocate for the Arab Peace Initiative (API), which was adopted in 2002 by the Arab League and offers comprehensive peace based on the principles of international law, United Nations resolutions, and the establishment of a viable Palestinian state with East Jerusalem as its capital.

The initiative not only emphasises the need for a just resolution to the Israeli-Palestinian conflict but also provides a framework for regional peace and normalisation of relations between Arab states and Israel. Furthermore, the kingdom has consistently criticised Israeli policies, particularly regarding settlements in the West Bank and the blockade on the Gaza Strip, deeming them as obstacles to achieving a meaningful resolution to the conflict.

To support its stance on the Israeli-Palestinian conflict, Saudi Arabia has implemented various methods of influence. The kingdom has provided financial aid to Palestinians, contributing to development projects, humanitarian assistance, and infrastructure development. These efforts aim to alleviate the suffering of the Palestinian people and improve their living conditions, while also reinforcing Saudi Arabia's commitment to their cause. Additionally, Saudi Arabia has utilised its influence within the Arab world to garner support for the Palestinian cause and rally Arab states behind a unified position. By leveraging its regional status, the kingdom fosters collective action and strengthens the bargaining power of the Arab states in engaging with Israel and the international community.

However, several factors limit Saudi Arabia's influence in the Israeli-Palestinian conflict. One formidable constraint is its relationship with the United States. The kingdom maintains a crucial alliance with the U.S., which not only provides Riyadh with stability and security guarantees but also shapes its approach to the conflict. Recognising the immense influence of the U.S. in the region and its role as a key mediator, Saudi Arabia often treads with caution to avoid strained relations and potential repercussions that may jeopardise its critical alliance. While the kingdom may privately express criticism over certain U.S. policies or decisions, it often seeks balanced rhetoric to maintain harmony diplomatically. Additionally, the United States has historically played a pivotal role in Israeli-Palestinian negotiations, and as such, Saudi Arabia has sought to cooperate and align its actions with U.S. initiatives, both to maintain its alliance and to ensure its perspectives are considered in the peace process.

Another factor that significantly impacts Saudi Arabia's influence is the broader regional power dynamics in the Middle East. Saudi Arabia remains locked in a fierce rivalry with Iran, each vying for regional dominance and influence. This rivalry stretches beyond the Israeli-Palestinian conflict and permeates various geopolitical arenas in the region. Iran's staunch support for Palestinian militant groups, such as Hamas and Islamic Jihad, often complicates Saudi efforts for peace and stability. As the kingdom seeks to counter Iran's regional actions and mitigate its influence, its efforts to effectively mediate or influence the Israeli-Palestinian conflict encounter significant headwinds. Iran's involvement fuels tension, hinders dialogue, and perpetuates the cycle of violence in the region. Saudi Arabia finds itself in a precarious position, balancing its support for the Palestinian cause alongside its efforts to confront Iranian interference and maintain regional stability.

Furthermore, internal challenges within Saudi Arabia also affect its position on the Israeli-Palestinian conflict. The kingdom is a diverse society with varying degrees of religious, political, and ideological perspectives. While the Saudi government may express support for a more conciliatory approach towards Israel, elements within the conservative segments of society may resist such changes. Saudi society, deeply connected to the Palestinian cause, holds a longstanding commitment to the Palestinian struggle, resulting in potential domestic opposition to any perceived concessions or shifts in the kingdom's stance. Balancing public sentiment, while pursuing strategic foreign policy objectives, poses a challenge for Saudi decision-makers. Despite the initiatives undertaken by the Saudi leadership to modernise and liberalise the country, there remains a delicate balance to be struck between societal expectations and the pursuit of political objectives in relation to the Israeli-Palestinian conflict.

Additionally, Saudi Arabia's own security concerns significantly limit its influence in the Israeli-Palestinian conflict. As a nation at the heart of the Muslim world, the kingdom maintains an acute awareness of its regional security landscape. A destabilised Palestine undermines the stability of the broader region and poses consequential risks to Saudi Arabia. Potential spillover effects from the conflict, such as radicalisation, increased terrorism, and broader sectarian tensions, are seen as threats that may directly impact Saudi Arabia's security interests. Consequently, the kingdom endeavours to contribute to a peaceful resolution to mitigate these risks and safeguard its own stability. By advocating for a just and comprehensive peace, Saudi Arabia seeks to ensure an environment that reduces the potential for violence and extremism, thereby fostering regional security and ultimately safeguarding its interests.

In conclusion, Saudi Arabia's position in the Israeli-Palestinian conflict is multifaceted and influenced by a complex interaction of factors. While the kingdom has historically voiced unequivocal support for Palestinian rights and a comprehensive peace solution, its relationship with the United States, regional power dynamics, domestic pressures, and security concerns all contribute to the limitations on its ability to influence the conflict. Navigating these challenges adequately is essential for Saudi Arabia to effectively contribute to the resolution of the Israeli-Palestinian conflict and foster lasting peace in the region. Through engaging in diplomatic initiatives, supporting Palestinian development, and aligning its policies with regional stability, Saudi Arabia strives to play a constructive role in seeking a durable and just solution for both Israelis and Palestinians alike.

Chapter 20

Somalia's Involvement and the Difficulties It Encounters

S omalia, a country located in the Horn of Africa, has long been grappling with its own internal struggles, ranging from political instability to terrorism and recurring humanitarian crises. These internal issues have greatly impacted Somalia's ability to actively engage in resolving the Israeli-Palestinian conflict and have shaped its limited involvement in the broader Middle East affairs.

One of the primary difficulties Somalia encounters is the lack of a functional and unified central government. Since the overthrow of Siad Barre's regime in 1991, Somalia has been engulfed in a state of protracted conflict, characterised by clan rivalries, warlordism, and a constant struggle for power, resulting in a fragmented political landscape. The absence of a stable government hinders Somalia's capacity to effectively participate in diplomatic efforts and provide substantial support to Palestine. The country's long road towards political reconciliation and state-building has been marred by continuous wrangling between various regions and groups vying for influence. As Somalia works towards achieving political stability and consensus among its fractured society, it is challenging for the nation to actively partake in mediating the Israeli-Palestinian conflict. The establishment of a robust central government that represents the interests of all Somalis is paramount to advancing Somalia's role in the Israeli-Palestinian peace process.

Furthermore, Somalia's security situation remains a significant concern. The country has been plagued by the presence of al-Shabaab, an extremist group linked to Al-Qaeda, which has engaged in acts of terrorism and insurgency. Al-Shabaab's influence and control over certain areas have limited Somalia's ability to allocate resources and attention to external conflicts, including the Israeli-Palestinian issue. The group's tactics include suicide bombings, guerrilla warfare, and targeted assassinations, aimed not only at destabilising Somalia but also at discouraging the nation from engaging in regional conflicts. These security threats compound the challenges Somalia faces in extending its involvement in the Gaza crisis. The Somali government must prioritise tackling terrorism and insurgency within its borders to create a conducive environment for engaging in broader regional issues.

Another significant challenge faced by Somalia is its economic crisis. The country has been grappling with widespread poverty, limited infrastructure, and a lack of basic services that significantly affect the livelihoods of its citizens. Decades of conflict and political instability have hindered economic growth and left the majority of Somalis struggling to meet their basic needs. Unemployment rates are alarmingly high, and resources are primarily directed towards addressing immediate domestic needs rather than allocating financial support to Palestine or investing in diplomatic avenues to influence the conflict positively. The economic strain in Somalia significantly limits the extent to which the country can contribute to the resolution of the Israeli-Palestinian conflict. To actively participate in the peace process, Somalia must prioritise economic development, attract foreign investments, and foster sustainable growth for its population.

Additionally, Somalia's geographical location poses further obstacles to its involvement in the Israeli-Palestinian conflict. Situated on the eastern coast of Africa, Somalia is geographically distant from the Middle East. The geographic distance limits direct engagement and the ease of coordinating efforts with other Arab states or international players involved in resolving the Gaza crisis. Somalia's physical separation diminishes its ability to directly impact the conflict's dynamics and poses logistical challenges when seeking to exert influence or provide support in person. Nevertheless, the advancement of digital communication and technology presents opportunities for Somalia to bridge this gap and participate in diplomatic negotiations remotely.

Despite these challenges, Somalia has shown some level of engagement in addressing the Israeli-Palestinian conflict. The Somali government has occasionally expressed solidarity with Palestine and condemned Israeli actions in Gaza, primarily through statements and resolutions issued by the Ministry of Foreign Affairs. These expressions of support have had limited practical impact due to the aforementioned constraints. Furthermore, Somalia occasionally participates in international forums where the Israeli-Palestinian conflict is discussed, providing insights from its own experiences with conflict resolution and state-building. By actively participating in diplomatic discussions and sharing its unique perspectives, Somalia can contribute to shaping the narrative and advocating for a just and lasting peace in the region.

In conclusion, Somalia's involvement in the Israeli-Palestinian conflict is significantly hampered by internal instability, security concerns, economic challenges, and geographical distance. While Somalia recognises the plight of Palestinians and shares their aspirations for self-determination, the country's focus remains primarily on grappling with its own pressing issues. To effectively address the Gaza crisis, it is crucial for Somalia to first achieve internal stability and rebuild its institutions. Only then can it play a more active and influential role in mediating the conflict and supporting Palestine's cause. The international community should continue to support Somalia's peace-building efforts and work towards creating an environment conducive to Somalia's enhanced engagement in regional affairs.

Chapter 21

Sudan's Stance and the Pressures That Constrain Its Actions

S udan, a country located in north-eastern Africa, has faced numerous challenges in addressing the Israeli-Palestinian conflict and finding an effective stance. As a member of the Arab League and the Organisation of Islamic Cooperation, Sudan is expected to rally behind the Palestinian cause and advocate for its rights. However, internal pressures, a complex political landscape, historical context, economic constraints, and strategic alliances have all hindered Sudan's ability to take decisive action in the ongoing Gaza crisis.

Historically, Sudan has been a vocal supporter of the Palestinian cause, rooted in a shared Pan-Arab sentiment and the strong influence of Islam in the country. The Palestinian struggle resonates deeply with the Sudanese people, who see it as a continuation of their own liberation movements against colonial oppression. Sudan's empathy towards the Palestinians can be traced back to the Arab-Israeli wars, particularly the 1967 Six-Day War and the 1973 Yom Kippur War, which further solidified Sudan's position on Palestine as a key issue of regional importance. Sudan's condemnation of Israeli aggression and calls for the establishment of a viable Palestinian state have been consistent pillars of its foreign policy approach over the years.

However, Sudan's own internal struggles – noticeably, the ongoing internal war between armed factions, led by Al-Burhan on one side and Hemidti on the other - have limited its capacity to actively engage in resolving the Israeli-Palestinian conflict. The Darfur conflict, which erupted in 2003, and other ongoing conflicts within the country have strained the Sudanese government's resources, attention, and ability to project influence beyond its borders. The funds that would have otherwise been allocated to international diplomatic efforts or providing humanitarian aid often had to be redirected towards addressing these pressing domestic issues. Consequently, despite its strong rhetoric, Sudan's ability to contribute substantially to resolving the Gaza crisis has been compromised.

Furthermore, Sudan's political landscape and the complexities that come with it have significantly impacted its ability to take a firm stance on the Israeli-Palestinian conflict. Following the ousting of former President Omar al-Bashir in 2019, Sudan entered a period of political transition characterised by power struggles, competing factions, and a fragile balance of power. The reformation of governance structures, development of a new constitution, and the establishment of a civilian-led government have been top priorities during this transitional phase, leaving limited space for proactive engagement in the external realm, including the Israeli-Palestinian conflict. Managing and stabilising internal affairs has taken precedence, diverting attention from external conflicts.

Moreover, Sudan's relationships with regional powers and its alliances play a crucial role in shaping its stance on the Israeli-Palestinian conflict.

Sudan has historically had mixed relations with other Arab states and regional actors, often navigating a delicate balance between aligning with the Arab League's united front against Israel while maintaining pragmatic relationships with countries like Saudi Arabia, Egypt, and the United Arab Emirates. These complex dynamics create challenges for Sudan to adopt a coherent and consistent approach towards the Gaza crisis, as competing pressures and conflicting interests from various external actors have the potential to sway its actions.

Additionally, economic constraints have been a significant factor in constraining Sudan's actions in the Israeli-Palestinian conflict. For years, Sudan has grappled with widespread poverty, inflation, a shortage of foreign currency, and a debt crisis. The government has been preoccupied with addressing these domestic economic challenges, making it difficult to allocate sufficient resources for robust diplomatic initiatives and humanitarian aid efforts in support of the Palestinians. The economic constraints exacerbate the challenges faced by Sudan in playing a more proactive role in resolving the Gaza crisis on a practical level.

Despite these constraints, Sudan has previously recognised the importance of supporting the Palestinian cause and the same rhetoric of solidarity than other Arab countries, which costs nothing than words. Sudan's engagement with international efforts, such as participating in regional summits and supporting resolutions condemning Israeli aggression in international forums like the United Nations, showcases its dedication to the Palestinian cause. Sudan continues to call for the recognition of a sovereign Palestinian state with East Jerusalem as its capital, highlighting the need for a just and lasting resolution to the conflict.

In conclusion, Sudan faces numerous pressures that constrain its actions in the Israeli-Palestinian conflict, chief among them its recent relationships with Israel. Internal challenges, such as economic struggles and political transitions, divert attention and resources away from engaging effectively. External pressures, including complicated regional dynamics and alliances, further complicate Sudan's ability to take a decisive stance. The historical context, rooted in shared Pan-Arab sentiment, liberation struggles, and the influence of Islam, also shapes Sudan's position on the Palestinian cause. Nevertheless, Sudan acknowledges the significance of the Palestinian cause and continues to express solidarity, albeit with limited capacity to actively contribute towards its resolution. The ongoing tensions and complexities surrounding the Israeli-Palestinian conflict require nuanced diplomacy and strategic manoeuvring, which Sudan strives to engage in despite the constraints it faces.

Chapter 22

Syria's Role in the Israeli-Palestinian Conflict and Its Own Internal Struggles

S yria's involvement in the Israeli-Palestinian conflict has been extensive and complex, shaped by historical, geopolitical, domestic, and regional factors. Understanding Syria's role requires examining its support for the Palestinian cause, internal challenges, and the broader regional dynamics.

Syria's backing of the Palestinian cause can be traced back to its quest for pan-Arab leadership during the 20th century. The late President Hafez al-Assad, who ruled from 1970 to 2000, positioned Syria as a champion of the Palestinian national aspirations and consistently rallied against Israeli occupation. By supporting Palestinian factions such as Hamas and Islamic Jihad, providing a safe haven for Palestinian refugees, and advocating for their rights on various international platforms, Syria aimed to bolster its regional standing and gain influence in the Israeli-Palestinian conflict.

The Assad regime's commitment to the Palestinian cause continued under the leadership of Bashar al-Assad, who assumed power in 2000. Despite the challenges posed by the Arab Spring uprisings in 2011 and the subsequent civil war, Syria's support for the Palestinians remained relatively consistent. However, as the conflict escalated, the regime's ability to actively engage in external conflicts, including the Israeli-Palestinian conflict, became increasingly constrained.

The eruption of the Syrian civil war in 2011 reshaped the dynamics both within Syria and in its engagement with the Israeli-Palestinian conflict. The initial protests demanding political reforms quickly transformed into a multifaceted conflict involving various domestic and international actors. The Assad regime, facing opposition from diverse factions, resorted to brutal tactics to suppress the uprising, leading to widespread violence and a protracted humanitarian crisis.

The pressing need to maintain internal stability amid the civil war significantly limited Syria's capacity to shape the Israeli-Palestinian conflict. As resources were drained to address urgent domestic challenges, including addressing the country's crumbling infrastructure, providing minimal social services, and responding to the immense refugee crisis, Syria's engagement in external affairs declined. The Assad regime shifted its focus to securing its own survival, relying on military support from Russia and Iran to maintain control over strategically significant regions.

In addition to grappling with its internal struggles, Syria's involvement in the Israeli-Palestinian conflict has been intricately tied to broader regional dynamics. Syria's close alliance with Iran, which shares its support for Palestinian militant groups like Hamas, has fuelled tensions with Israel. The alliance with Iran has also facilitated the logistical and financial support of Hezbollah in Lebanon, presenting another front in the Israeli conflict. Syria has served as a geographic and strategic link for Iran's assistance to Hezbollah, making it a target for periodic Israeli airstrikes to disrupt this support network.

Moreover, Syria's diplomatic standing in the international community has suffered due to the civil war's brutal consequences. The Assad regime's alleged use of chemical weapons, indiscriminate targeting of civilian areas, and human rights abuses have caused widespread condemnation and international isolation. As a result, Syria has faced difficulties in effectively advocating for the Palestinian cause on the global stage and engaging in diplomatic efforts to find a resolution to the Israeli-Palestinian conflict.

The emergence of ISIS and other extremist groups in Syria further complicated the situation. Faced with the threat of terrorism within its borders, Syria diverted significant resources toward countering these extremist organisations. The fight against ISIS became a primary focus, causing a shift in Syria's priorities away from actively shaping the Israeli-Palestinian conflict. The battle against extremist groups has necessitated collaboration with multiple regional and international actors, altering the dynamics of Syria's engagement in external conflicts.

In conclusion, Syria's role in the Israeli-Palestinian conflict has been shaped by its historical support for the Palestinian cause, domestic struggles, and regional dynamics. The devastating civil war, international isolation, shifting power dynamics, and the emergence of extremist groups have significantly limited Syria's capacity to actively influence the course of the conflict. As Syria continues to grapple with its internal struggles and regional complexities, questions remain about its future role in the Israeli-Palestinian arena and whether it can regain its previous position as a key player in the pursuit of a just resolution.

Chapter 23

Tunisia's Position and the Challenges It Faces as a Transitional State

T unisia, known as the birthplace of the Arab Spring, has been un-dergoing a significant transition since the overthrow of its longtime autocratic leader in 2011. This chapter delves into Tunisia's stance and the challenges it faces in the complex Israeli-Palestinian conflict.

As a transitional state, Tunisia has had to navigate internal power strug-gles, political instability, and economic challenges since the revolution. This has posed obstacles to its ability to effectively engage in the Is-raeli-Palestinian conflict and find a suitable position that aligns with its own interests and values.

Tunisia's historical stance on the Israeli-Palestinian conflict has been one of support for the Palestinian cause. It has long advocated for the estab-lishment of an independent Palestinian state and has condemned Israeli actions, particularly its settlement expansion in the West Bank. Tunisia, home to one of the largest Palestinian communities in the region and a

strong pro-Palestinian sentiment among its population, has consistently voiced solidarity with the Palestinian people and their aspirations for
self-determination.

However, the transitional nature of the country has created complexities
in its ability to effectively address this issue. One of the key challenges
Tunisia faces is the need to consolidate its democratic institutions and
strengthen its political stability. The transition from an autocratic regime
to a democratic system has been marked by frequent changes in leadership,
disagreements among political parties, and a fragile balance of power.

The initial euphoria of political change in Tunisia quickly gave way to
political gridlock and the rise of regionalism. Different factions emerged
with varying political ideologies, some advocating a more assertive stance
against Israeli policies, while others prioritised stability and regional diplomacy. The prevalence of differing views has made it difficult for Tunisia to
form a unified and consistent position on the Israeli-Palestinian conflict.

Furthermore, Tunisia's economic struggles pose another significant
challenge. High unemployment rates, regional disparities, and social in-
equalities have been ongoing issues for the country. The economic situation has worsened in the aftermath of the revolution, with foreign
investment dwindling and a decline in tourism, which was once a vital
source of revenue. These economic challenges take precedence in Tunisia's
domestic agenda, limiting its capacity to actively engage in resolving the
Israeli-Palestinian conflict and provide meaningful support to Palestine.

Additionally, in its endeavour to navigate the complexities of domestic
politics and economic challenges, Tunisia faces the delicate task of maintaining a diplomatic balance. The country maintains relationships with
various regional and international actors, some of whom have differing

positions on the Israeli-Palestinian conflict. Tunisia must carefully navigate these relationships, weighing its desire to support the Palestinian cause against the need to secure economic assistance and investments. This balancing act often influences its ability to take a firm and consistent stance on the conflict.

Despite these challenges, Tunisia has made efforts to contribute to the resolution of the Israeli-Palestinian conflict. It has supported diplomatic initiatives, participated in international forums, and reaffirmed its commitment to a two-state solution. Tunisia has also hosted international conferences and facilitated dialogue between Israeli and Palestinian officials. These actions demonstrate Tunisia's willingness to play a constructive role in finding a peaceful solution.

However, the transitional nature of the country and the challenges it faces have somewhat limited its impact on the conflict. Tunisia's consolidation of democratic institutions, resolution of internal conflicts, and economic stability are prerequisites for it to play a more active role in resolving the Israeli-Palestinian conflict. The international community must also recognise Tunisia's unique position as a transitional state and provide the support necessary for the country to effectively engage in the peacemaking process.

Furthermore, Tunisia's own regional context cannot be ignored. The ongoing conflict in neighbouring Libya and the security threats posed by extremist groups have diverted Tunisia's attention and resources away from the Israeli-Palestinian conflict. Tunisia is also grappling with the repercussions of the Syrian civil war, which has led to an influx of refugees, straining its already fragile economy and social fabric.

Moreover, Tunisia's experience with political Islamism adds another layer of complexity to its position on the Israeli-Palestinian conflict. En-nahda, an Islamic-leaning political party, emerged as a leading force follow-ing the revolution and has maintained a significant influence over Tunisia's political landscape. While Ennahda has historically shown support for the Palestinian cause, its position within the broader context of political Islamism can shape Tunisia's approach to the Israeli-Palestinian conflict. Balancing domestic political considerations and regional dynamics further challenges Tunisia's ability to take a consistent stance.

In conclusion, Tunisia's position in the Israeli-Palestinian conflict is in-fluenced by its status as a transitional state facing internal power struggles, political instability, and economic challenges. While it maintains support for the Palestinian cause, its ability to effectively engage and make a signif-icant impact is hindered. Tunisia's consolidation of democratic institu-tions, resolution of internal conflicts, and economic stability are prereq-uisites for it to play a more active role in resolving the Israeli-Palestinian conflict. The international community must support Tunisia's efforts and recognise its unique position as a transitional state with valuable contri-butions to the quest for peace in the region. Additionally, acknowledging Tunisia's regional context and the complexities of political Islamism will provide a more comprehensive understanding of the challenges it faces in effectively addressing the Israeli-Palestinian conflict.

Chapter 24

United Arab Emirates' Approach and the Geopolitical Considerations

The United Arab Emirates (UAE) has adopted a unique approach towards the Israeli-Palestinian conflict, driven by a combination of geopolitical considerations, strategic goals, and historical context. This chapter delves extensively into the nuanced stance of the UAE, exploring the factors that shape its approach and the intricacies of its engagement with Israel and Palestine.

Geopolitically, the UAE recognises the evolving dynamics in the Middle East and aims to position itself as a key regional player. The country leverages its soft power to attract investments, build relationships, and cement its status as a hub for commerce, tourism, and diplomacy. By engaging with both Israel and Palestine, the UAE seeks to strengthen its network of alliances, extend its influence, and maintain an active role in shaping regional affairs.

Strategically, the UAE's approach to the Israeli-Palestinian conflict is heavily influenced by its concerns about Iran's regional ambitions. As Iran continues to assert its influence in various countries, the UAE perceives the need for alliances and partnerships to counterbalance this expansion. Collaborating with countries like Israel, which shares similar concerns about Iran, provides the UAE with opportunities for enhanced security cooperation and intelligence sharing, strengthening regional stability.

The historical context of the UAE also plays a role in its approach. The country has historically maintained relative detachment from the Is-raeli-Palestinian conflict, with its primary focus on domestic development and stability. This distance allows the UAE to approach the conflict prag-matically, unencumbered by deep-seated ideological positions, and explore avenues for dialogue and cooperation that lead to tangible outcomes.

Central to the UAE's approach is the belief in the power of dialogue and cooperation as vital tools for achieving peace. The country acknowledges that isolation and condemnation have yielded limited results in resolving the conflict, and thus seeks to engage with both Israel and Palestine to foster effective outcomes. This pragmatic viewpoint aligns with the UAE's broader vision of stability and prosperity in the Middle East, as well as its commitment to multilateralism and peaceful coexistence.

Nevertheless, the UAE's engagement with Israel has invited criticism from some quarters. Critics argue that by normalising relations, the UAE risks diluting the collective Arab stance on the Israeli-Palestinian conflict. They contend that such normalisation can be seen as acquiescing to Israel's occupation of Palestinian lands, potentially weakening the position of the Palestinians in future negotiations.

Despite the criticism, the UAE maintains that its engagement with Israel is aimed at promoting dialogue, finding practical solutions, and fostering positive change. The UAE emphasises the importance of addressing the root causes of the conflict and working towards a two-state solution that guarantees the rights and aspirations of both Israelis and Palestinians. It advocates for a halt to Israeli settlements, an end to violence, and negotiations based on international law and relevant United Nations resolutions.

To navigate the complex geopolitical considerations and criticism, the UAE has taken cautious steps in its engagement with Israel. The foundation of this engagement was laid through the historic Abraham Accords, which formalised diplomatic ties between the UAE and Israel. This normalisation paved the way for several initiatives to deepen economic, cultural, and technological cooperation between the two nations. These initiatives include the establishment of direct flights, the opening of embassies, and the promotion of people-to-people connections.

As the UAE continues to strengthen its relationship with Israel, it remains committed to supporting efforts to resolve the Israeli-Palestinian conflict and achieve a just and lasting peace. The country encourages dialogue between Israelis and Palestinians, recognising that a sustainable resolution requires direct negotiations and mutual recognition of each other's legitimate aspirations. The UAE supports international initiatives, including the Quartet-led peace process, that aim to bring the parties back to the negotiating table and advance a comprehensive, negotiated settlement.

In conclusion, the UAE's approach to the Israeli-Palestinian conflict is shaped by a combination of geopolitical considerations, strategic goals, and historical context. As the UAE positions itself as a key player in the region, it engages with both Israel and Palestine to consolidate alliances, address security concerns, and foster peace through pragmatic means. While facing criticism, the UAE maintains that its approach contributes to the broader objective of a just and lasting resolution to the conflict, underpinned by dialogue, cooperation, and respect for international law and relevant resolutions.

Chapter 25

Yemen's Challenges in Addressing the Gaza Crisis

Yemen, a country located on the southern tip of the Arabian Peninsula, faces numerous challenges in effectively addressing the Gaza crisis. The complexities and difficulties Yemen encounters stem from its internal conflicts, ongoing civil war, humanitarian crisis, geographic location, and regional dynamics.

Since 2014, Yemen has been embroiled in a multifaceted conflict. The Houthi rebels, an armed group representing a predominantly Shia Muslim sect, seized control of the capital, Sana'a, and large parts of the country, triggering a military intervention led by a coalition of Arab states, primarily spearheaded by Saudi Arabia and the United Arab Emirates. This internal strife, along with political fragmentation and competing interests, has hindered Yemen's ability to allocate resources towards addressing external conflicts, including the long-standing Israeli-Palestinian issue.

The internal dynamics of Yemen's conflict further complicate its engagement in the Gaza crisis. The Houthi rebels, who originated from the northern Saada province, have adopted an anti-Israel stance that aligns with Iran's regional ambitions. Their emphasis on the Palestinian cause serves as a rallying cry to foster Iranian support and gain legitimacy among other regional actors who champion the Palestinian cause. This alignment has the potential to both complicate and polarise Yemen's efforts to contribute to a peaceful resolution.

The humanitarian crisis in Yemen presents another significant challenge. The ongoing conflict has compounded pre-existing issues, plunging the country into one of the world's worst humanitarian disasters. Continuous violence, attacks on civilian infrastructure, and obstruction of humanitarian aid have resulted in widespread displacement, food insecurity, and a collapsing healthcare system. Yemenis are grappling with limited access to clean water, sanitation facilities, and healthcare services. The urgent need to alleviate these domestic challenges places further strain on Yemen's capacity to actively engage in resolving the Gaza crisis.

Furthermore, Yemen's geographic location presents obstacles to its involvement in the Israeli-Palestinian conflict. Situated on the opposite side of the Arabian Peninsula from Palestine, physical distance limits Yemen's direct engagement in negotiations and renders immediate assistance challenging. However, despite the geographical gap, Yemen maintains diplomatic relations with Palestine and has expressed solidarity with the Palestinian cause. Yemen's involvement primarily lies in the form of diplomatic support, primarily through the Arab League and international platforms, where it advocates for the rights and interests of Palestinians.

Yemen's relationship with Saudi Arabia, a key player in the Israeli-Palestinian conflict and the wider region, affects its approach to addressing the Gaza crisis. Saudi Arabia has been actively involved in supporting the government in Yemen's civil war, leading the military coalition against the Houthi rebels. While Yemen may have concerns related to the Saudi-led intervention, it remains mindful of maintaining a delicate balance to sustain much-needed support and assistance. Negotiating this complex regional dynamic compels Yemen to tread cautiously, as its primary focus remains on its domestic challenges.

Furthermore, Yemen's limited economic resources constrain its ability to engage actively in the resolution of conflicts beyond its borders. The civil war, coupled with economic decline, has severely hampered the country's financial capacity to contribute significantly to relief efforts and regional initiatives tackling the Israeli-Palestinian conflict. Yemen's internal conflicts have drained its resources, leaving little to spare for international engagement, resulting in a lack of financial contributions to support Palestinian causes.

Despite these challenges, Yemen's cultural and historical ties to the Palestinian cause provide a foundation for continued support. Yemen, a predominantly Sunni Muslim country, has a long-standing tradition of supporting the rights of Palestinians against occupation and oppression. Its people often demonstrate solidarity with protests, sending aid, and advocating for the Palestinian cause through various non-governmental organisations and civil society groups. While their contributions may not be on a grand scale, the grassroots support demonstrates Yemen's commitment and empathy towards the struggles faced by Palestinians.

In conclusion, Yemen faces a myriad of challenges in effectively addressing the Gaza crisis. Internal conflicts, a dire humanitarian situation, geographic constraints, and complex regional dynamics all culminate in limiting Yemen's capacity to play an active role in resolving the Israeli-Palestinian conflict. Despite expressing unwavering solidarity with Palestine,

Yemen is hampered by multifaceted obstacles. As the country continues to grapple with internal strife and debilitating humanitarian challenges, Yemen's ability to contribute meaningfully to peace efforts in Gaza remains significantly constrained. Nonetheless, Yemen's cultural ties and grassroots support for Palestine provide a glimmer of hope for future engagement if they can overcome these formidable obstacles.

Chapter 26

Analysis of the Pressures and Problems Faced by Arab States in Achieving a Cease-fire

I n the midst of the Israeli-Palestinian conflict, Arab states have been grappling with numerous pressures and problems as they strive to achieve a meaningful cease-fire and restore much-needed peace in the region. The intricacies of the conflict combined with internal and external challenges have made this task exceedingly complex and arduous.

One of the significant pressures faced by Arab states is the internal division among themselves regarding their approach to the conflict. Arab states have historically held differing ideologies and tactics when it comes to dealing with Israel. Some countries, such as Egypt and Jordan, have chosen to pursue peace treaties and diplomatic engagement with Israel. These countries argue that peaceful negotiations are the most viable means to address the conflict and achieve a two-state solution. On the other hand, countries like Iran and Syria favour a more aggressive stance, seeking to confront and challenge Israeli policies directly. They argue that only by resisting and exerting pressure on Israel can the Palestinian cause be advanced and the occupation be brought to an end. This fragmentation within the Arab world undermines their ability to present a united front, exert collective influence, and effectively advocate for their desired course of action in achieving a cease-fire agreement.

Additionally, Arab states face external pressures emanating from various international powers. The United States has historically played a significant role in mediating the conflict, often favouring Israel due to its close alliance. Other influential players like Russia, the European Union, and regional powers such as Iran and Turkey also seek to shape the outcome of the conflict according to their interests. These powers, motivated by their own vested interests and agendas, often exert their influence to advance their own goals rather than promoting a fair and just resolution to the conflict. This external influence dilutes the impact and effectiveness of Arab states, as they are subjected to the interests and intentions of external actors. The competitive geopolitical dynamics observed in the region further exacerbate this issue, as global powers vie for influence and control, potentially hijacking the peace process to serve their own strategic ends.

Another challenge faced by Arab states is the significant power asymmetry between themselves and Israel. Israel, backed by substantial military and economic support from the United States, enjoys strong military capabilities, advanced technologies, and economic prosperity. This advantage renders it difficult for Arab states, many of which suffer from insufficient military capacities and limited economic resources, to exert significant pressure or influence on Israel. The power imbalance gives Israel the ability to dictate terms in negotiations, shape the narrative surrounding the conflict, and imposes limitations on the leverage Arab states possess. This, in turn, significantly impacts their ability to achieve a just and lasting cease-fire agreement, diminishing their capacity to ensure a fair resolution of the conflict.

Furthermore, the historical grievances and deep-rooted animosity between Israel and several Arab states add an additional layer of complexity to the conflict resolution process. Decades of unresolved issues, territorial disputes, and conflicting narratives have contributed to a trust deficit and a sense of victimhood among Palestinians and Arab states. The establishment of the state of Israel in 1948, alongside the subsequent displacement and suffering of Palestinians, has left deep scars in the collective memory of the Arab world. These historical grievances coupled with ongoing Israeli settlement expansion, the construction of the separation wall, and human rights violations against Palestinians fuel resentment and hinder the prospects for a peaceful resolution. This trust gap makes it challenging for Arab states to broker meaningful negotiations and achieve a mutually acceptable cease-fire agreement. Overcoming these historical grievances requires a robust commitment from all parties involved to engage in a comprehensive dialogue that addresses the root causes of the conflict.

Moreover, the internal political dynamics within Arab states themselves can impede progress towards a cease-fire. In some countries, longstanding conflicts or tensions between different factions or groups within society take precedence, diverting attention and resources away from the larger Israeli-Palestinian conflict. The rise of sectarianism, such as in Iraq and Lebanon, as well as political instability, like in Libya and Yemen, create distractions and hinder Arab states' efforts to address the Israeli-Palestinian issue effectively. These internal divisions not only weaken the bargaining power of Arab states but also allow external actors to exploit these vulnerabilities, further complicating the path to peace.

Economic considerations also play a significant role in determining the approach of Arab states towards the cease-fire. Many countries in the Arab region already face economic challenges, including high unemployment rates, limited resources, and pressing domestic priorities. The allocation of significant resources towards resolving the Israeli-Palestinian conflict may strain their budgets, impacting their development plans and their ability to address pressing needs in their own societies. This financial pressure can limit their ability to engage fully and effectively in the peace process, adding another layer of complexity to the pursuit of a cease-fire agreement.

Lastly, the lack of a clear and unified strategy among Arab states further complicates the path to achieving a cease-fire. While individual countries may have their own strategies, priorities, and alliances, the absence of a cohesive and comprehensive approach weakens their position and allows other actors to manipulate the situation to their advantage. Arab states must bridge their differences and adopt a unified stance to have a meaningful impact on the peace process.

In conclusion, Arab states face a multitude of pressures and problems in their pursuit of a cease-fire in the Israeli-Palestinian conflict. Internal divisions, external pressures, power asymmetry, historical grievances, economic considerations, political instability, and the lack of a unified strategy all contribute to the complexity of the situation. Overcoming these challenges will require a united and coordinated effort among Arab states, coupled with international support and a comprehensive approach that addresses the root causes of the conflict. Only through such concerted efforts can a just and lasting peace be achieved in the region.

Chapter 27

Identifying the Marginalisation of Arab States in the Israeli-Palestinian Conflict

The Israeli-Palestinian conflict remains one of the most enduring and complex conflicts in the world. Efforts to find a peaceful resolution have involved numerous international actors, including Arab states. However, a closer examination reveals a recurring pattern of marginalisation endured by these Arab states in the context of the Israeli-Palestinian conflict. Delving deeper into the subject reveals several key factors that contribute to this marginalisation, shedding light on the intricate dynamics at play.

One fundamental factor that leads to the marginalisation of Arab states in the Israeli-Palestinian conflict is the historical power imbalance between Israel and the Arab world. Following the establishment of Israel in 1948, Arab states found themselves facing a militarily well-equipped nation with strong alliances, such as its relationship with the United States. This power disparity, coupled with Israel's demonstrated military capabilities during conflicts such as the Six-Day War (1967) and the Yom Kippur War (1973), has allowed Israel to exert significant influence over the conflict. Arab states, on the other hand, have often struggled to present a united front due to internal divisions and competing interests. This fragmentation undermines their capacity to effectively assert their interests, thereby marginalising their role in the peace process.

Moreover, the United States' involvement in the Israeli-Palestinian conflict has played a critical role in the marginalisation of Arab states. Historically, the U.S. has maintained a close alliance with Israel, providing extensive military, diplomatic, and financial support. This alignment has entrenched an asymmetry of power, where Arab states often find themselves overshadowed and undermined in efforts to find a peaceful resolution. The U.S.'s influential position in the conflict is further bolstered by its veto power in the United Nations Security Council. Resolutions critical of Israel face significant challenges, reinforcing the marginalisation of Arab states on the global stage.

Another essential element to consider is the historical legacy of the conflict, which significantly influences the marginalisation of Arab states. The establishment of Israel in 1948 resulted in profound displacement and dispossession for the Palestinian people. These historical grievances have engendered deep-rooted tensions that continue to shape the conflict. Arab states that were involved in past wars with Israel, such as Egypt, Syria, and Jordan, have faced difficulties in finding a common ground for negotiations due to the historical narratives and collective memory associated with these conflicts. Furthermore, the perception of Israel as a powerful military force has often discouraged Arab states from taking more assertive measures, leading to a sense of powerlessness and marginalisation.

Shifting regional dynamics also contribute to the marginalisation of Arab states in the Israeli-Palestinian conflict. The Middle East has witnessed a series of significant conflicts, including the ongoing wars in Syria, Yemen, and Iraq. Additionally, the rise of non-state actors such as ISIS and Hezbollah, with their own distinct agendas, has further complicated the regional landscape. These challenges place a strain on the resources and attention of Arab states, diverting their focus away from the Israeli-Palestinian conflict. As a result, Arab states find themselves with limited capacity to influence the peace process effectively, exacerbating their marginalisation.

Internal politics within Arab states also play a role in their marginalisation in the Israeli-Palestinian conflict. Leaders often prioritise political stability and regime survival, especially in the face of domestic challenges. Consequently, they may be reluctant to expend political capital on the Israeli-Palestinian issue, particularly when it does not directly align with their immediate domestic priorities. Furthermore, some leaders have exploited the conflict as a diversionary tactic, deflecting attention from internal issues. This instrumentalization of the conflict further marginalises its significance on the regional stage.

The media landscape also plays a crucial role in perpetuating the marginalisation of Arab states in the Israeli-Palestinian conflict. The predominance of Western media outlets and the bias often displayed in their coverage can influence public opinion and shape narratives. Arab states have struggled to effectively counter these narratives and present their perspective on the conflict to a global audience. The limited media representation and the resultant lack of information about the efforts made by Arab states to advance the peace process contribute to their marginalisation.

Further exacerbating the marginalisation of Arab states is the lack of Arab-Israeli normalisation agreements. While Egypt and Jordan have signed peace treaties with Israel, the vast majority of Arab states have yet to establish formal diplomatic ties. This absence of normalisation agreements limits their ability to directly engage with Israel on matters related to the Israeli-Palestinian conflict. By excluding Arab states from this avenue of communication and negotiation, their influence and agency in the conflict are further diminished.

In conclusion, a comprehensive understanding of the marginalisation of Arab states in the Israeli-Palestinian conflict requires a deeper exploration of the contributing factors. The power imbalance between Israel and the Arab world, the influence of the United States, historical grievances, shifting regional dynamics, internal political considerations, media bias, and the lack of Arab-Israeli normalisation agreements all shape the marginalisation of Arab states. Recognising and addressing these complex dynamics is crucial for Arab states to reclaim agency and play a meaningful role in the pursuit of a just and lasting peace in the region.

Chapter 28

Uncovering the Strings: Who Manipulates the Political Landscape?

T he Israeli-Palestinian conflict is a multifaceted puzzle that goes beyond the rivalry between two nations. At its core, it is a complex web of political manoeuvres, international alliances, and power plays. In this chapter, we will delve into the hidden forces and actors that manipulate the political landscape surrounding this enduring dispute, aiming to shed light on the intricate dynamics at play.

One cannot fully comprehend the Israeli-Palestinian conflict without acknowledging the significant influence exerted by external actors. Numerous countries, international organisations, and non-state entities have played pivotal roles, often pursuing their own interests rather than prioritising the resolution of the conflict itself.

The United States, for instance, has historically aligned itself firmly with

Israel, providing unwavering political, financial, and military support. This strategic partnership has propelled Israel to a position of strength in the international arena, significantly tilting the balance of power in its favour. Leveraging its diplomatic clout, the U.S. has asserted itself as a major player in the quest for a resolution, occasionally taking the lead in facilitating peace negotiations. However, critics argue that this close alignment undermines the neutrality of the United States, making it difficult to act as an impartial mediator.

But beyond diplomatic and military support, the influence of the United States goes even deeper. The pro-Israel lobby in the United States is incredibly powerful, particularly the American Israel Public Affairs Committee (AIPAC). AIPAC uses its considerable financial resources, connections, and political influence to shape US policy towards Israel. It mobilises its vast network of supporters to influence lawmakers, providing funding to political campaigns and organising trips to Israel for members of Congress.

Similarly, other countries in the region have sought to influence the political landscape surrounding the Israeli-Palestinian conflict. Iran, Saudi Arabia, and Turkey, among others, have employed their financial resources, religious affiliations, and regional connections to steer the dynamics of the conflict. Iran, motivated by its anti-Israel ideology and aspirations for regional dominance, has utilised proxy groups like Hezbollah to exert influence in Lebanon and challenge Israel's security. It fuels anti-Israel sentiment across the region and supports extremist groups that carry out attacks against Israel. Saudi Arabia, meanwhile, has pursued its own diplomatic initiatives, advocating for the Arab Peace Initiative and leveraging its economic leverage in an attempt to rally Arab states behind a comprehensive peace agreement. It wields its influence through economic support, investments, and political alliances, all aimed at advancing its own interests while ostensibly championing the Palestinian cause. Turkey, on the other hand, has positioned itself as a champion of the Palestinian cause, aiming to assert its regional leadership and bolster its influence among Muslim nations. It actively supports Palestinian political groups and provides humanitarian aid to the Palestinian territories.

Moreover, international organisations such as the United Nations, the European Union, and the Arab League have played significant roles in shaping the discourse and attempting to broker peace in the Israeli-Palestinian conflict. While the United Nations has issued numerous resolutions condemning Israeli actions, critics argue that the organisation's bias towards the Palestinian cause undermines its effectiveness as an impartial mediator. They believe that the disproportionate focus on Israel's actions undermines the peace process and perpetuates a one-sided narrative. The European Union, aiming to promote dialogue and diplomacy, has provided diplomatic and financial support to both parties, seeking to foster a climate conducive to peace. Its financial assistance, coupled with its position as an important trade partner, gives it some leverage over both Israel and the Palestinian Authority. The Arab League, representing the collective voice of Arab nations, has also used its platform to advocate for Palestinian rights and mobilise Arab support for their cause. The Arab League has provided financial aid and political backing to the Palestinians while also maintaining pressure on Israel through regional alliances.

Non-state actors, such as powerful lobby groups and grassroots organisations, have undeniably influenced the political landscape surrounding the Israeli-Palestinian conflict. Pro-Israel and pro-Palestinian organisations in the United States and other countries have tirelessly worked to shape public opinion, challenge policies, and influence decision-makers. These groups often possess significant financial resources and political connections, enabling them to exert considerable influence on the political process. Lobby groups like J Street, which advocates for a diplomatic approach to the Israeli-Palestinian conflict, have skillfully worked within the American political system to advocate for their respective positions. They provide a counterbalance to the influence of AIPAC, pushing for a more balanced US policy towards Israel. On the other hand, organisations like the Boycott, Divestment, and Sanctions (BDS) movement have garnered support for their efforts to pressure Israel economically and politically. BDS campaigns promote boycotts of Israeli products, divestment from companies doing business with Israel, and sanctions against the Israeli government, aiming to hold Israel accountable for its actions.

Furthermore, media organisations and journalists play a crucial role in shaping public perception of the conflict. Biases, misinformation, and sensationalism in media coverage can sway public opinion and, in turn, influence the political landscape. Critiques at times emerge concerning the media's impartiality, with assertions of biased reporting favouring one side or the other. Media outlets often play into pre-existing narratives and employ sensationalism to capture attention, potentially hindering constructive dialogue and understanding. However, alternative media outlets and independent journalists have emerged, seeking to provide a more nuanced and balanced perspective on the Israeli-Palestinian conflict. These sources provide critical analysis, fact-checking, and more comprehensive coverage that challenges the mainstream narrative.

Uncovering the strings that manipulate the political landscape surrounding the Israeli-Palestinian conflict requires vigilance and meticulous analysis. It is essential to question the motivations, interests, and influence of the various actors involved. By delving deeper into these key players and understanding the ways in which they manipulate the political landscape, we can gain a clearer understanding of the intricate dynamics at play, ultimately striving towards a more balanced and just resolution to this long-standing dispute.

Chapter 29

Socio-economic Factors Impacting Arab States' Influence on the Gaza Conflict

T he Israeli-Palestinian conflict is a multifaceted issue intertwined with socio-economic factors that heavily impact the actions and policies of Arab states in the region. In this extended chapter, we will delve deeper into these factors to acquire a comprehensive understanding of their influence on the Gaza conflict.

Economic Interests:

Economic interests play a central role in shaping Arab states' approach to the Israeli-Palestinian conflict. The stability and resolution of this conflict directly affect trade routes, investments, and economic cooperation. Arab states recognise the potential benefits that could arise from a peaceful resolution, as it would unlock economic opportunities and create a more conducive environment for regional trade.

Egypt, for example, shares a border with Gaza, making it a key player in efforts to mediate and ease tensions. Moreover, Egypt has a vested economic interest in the region, as the reopening of the Rafah border crossing would facilitate trade and strengthen ties between the Sinai Peninsula and Gaza. The Sinai Peninsula has the potential for economic development, with its tourism industry and natural gas reserves offering opportunities for growth and collaboration. However, the ongoing conflict restricts the realisation of these economic potentials.

Similarly, Jordan seeks stability in the region, as any escalation in the Gaza conflict would burden its already strained economy. As one of the closest Arab states to the Israeli-Palestinian conflict, Jordan shoulders the responsibility of hosting a significant number of Palestinian refugees. This influx has placed a strain on the country's resources and economy, making a resolution to the conflict a priority.

Saudi Arabia plays a prominent role in the Israeli-Palestinian conflict due to its influence in the Arab world and its position as a major regional economic powerhouse. The kingdom, driven by economic interests, seeks regional stability to promote investments and trade. Additionally, Saudi Arabia has a strong relationship with the United States, which plays a crucial role in mediation efforts and shaping the broader international response to the conflict.

Domestic Politics:

Domestic politics within each Arab state significantly influence their stance on the Gaza conflict. Public opinion, shaped by societal structures, cultural factors, and historical experiences, plays a decisive role in determining the government's approach. Arab leaders must navigate the delicate balance between external pressures and domestic interests to maintain stability and legitimacy. They must align their policies on the conflict with the aspirations and expectations of their citizens, ensuring they remain responsive to popular sentiment while pursuing their national interest.

In recent years, there has been an increasing emphasis by Arab states on soft power initiatives aimed at asserting cultural and political influence in the region. This includes the utilisation of media, cultural exports, and religious diplomacy to shape narratives concerning the Israeli-Palestinian conflict. With the rise of social media, public opinion in Arab states has become more influential, forcing governments to be more responsive and adopt a more proactive approach in addressing the conflict.

Furthermore, democratic movements and uprisings in the Arab world, such as the Arab Spring, have had a profound impact on domestic politics. These events have heightened the focus on the Israeli-Palestinian conflict, with protestors demanding their governments take a stronger stance against Israeli policies. The pressure from the populace has forced leaderships to reevaluate their positions and take a more assertive approach regarding the conflict.

Regional Alliances:

Arab states have historically formed alliances and coalitions to enhance their collective influence on regional conflicts, including the Israeli-Palestinian conflict. These alliances, such as the Arab League and the Gulf Cooperation Council (GCC), provide an avenue for Arab states to align their policies and coordinate actions, ultimately forming a united front in addressing the conflict.

The Arab League, formed in 1945, has played a prominent role in advocating for the rights of Palestinians and addressing the Israeli-Palestinian conflict. Its members have collectively supported a two-state solution, condemned Israeli settlements, and called for the establishment of an independent Palestinian state. However, the effectiveness of the Arab League has often been hindered by internal divisions and differing interests among its member states. Disagreements over approaches to the conflict, such as the use of economic and diplomatic pressure or the adoption of a more confrontational stance, have led to inconsistent actions and limited progress.

The GCC, consisting of six Arab states in the Persian Gulf region, also plays a significant role in shaping the policies of its member states regarding the Gaza conflict. With a focus on regional security and stability, the GCC states have sought to maintain good relations with major global powers, such as the United States, while also emphasising the importance of resolving the Israeli-Palestinian conflict. However, the GCC's influence varies depending on the individual member state and their particular geopolitical considerations.

Humanitarian Concerns:

The humanitarian crisis resulting from the Israeli-Palestinian conflict resonates strongly within the Arab world, shaping Arab states' actions and policies with regard to Gaza. Arab states often act as advocates for humanitarian aid, engage in diplomatic efforts, and provide financial support for relief projects.

Qatar has emerged as a key player in providing humanitarian assistance to Gaza. Through its support for reconstruction projects, the Qatari government contributes to alleviating the dire human suffering and addressing the severe shortage of infrastructure and basic services. Qatar also plays an important role in mediating between Hamas, the dae facto governing authority in Gaza, and other regional and international actors. Its financial support ensures the provision of essential services and plays a significant role in preventing an even greater humanitarian catastrophe.

Similarly, Egypt has consistently played a critical role in mediating cease-fires and facilitating humanitarian aid to Gaza. Despite political differences with Hamas, Egypt recognises the urgency of addressing the humanitarian crisis and has repeatedly exerted efforts to broker agreements, ensuring the flow of essential goods and services into the region. The Egyptian government also recognises that the alleviation of the humanitarian crisis is directly tied to enhancing stability in its own border regions.

International Relations:

The international relations of Arab states significantly influence their influence on the Gaza conflict. Factors such as trade agreements, alliances, and security arrangements with global powers can shape the stance of individual Arab states. Arab states, particularly those in the Persian Gulf region, have strengthened their ties with the United States and European countries, which may impact their ability to pursue independent strategies in resolving the conflict.

The relationship between Arab states and the United States has, historically, played a significant role in shaping the dynamics of the Israeli-Palestinian conflict. The United States has been the primary mediator between Israel and the Palestinians, often influencing the positions and policies of Arab states. The influence of the United States on Arab states can range from economic aid and military support to political pressure to engage in peace negotiations.

Furthermore, the geopolitical landscape of the broader Middle East also influences the approaches of Arab states towards the Israeli-Palestinian conflict. For instance, Iran's regional ambitions and rivalry with Arab states such as Saudi Arabia and the United Arab Emirates have led to a convergence of interests between Israel and these Arab states, resulting in a realignment of alliances and a more pragmatic approach to the conflict.

In conclusion, socio-economic factors constitute a fundamental aspect shaping the influence of Arab states on the Israeli-Palestinian conflict, particularly in relation to Gaza. Economic interests, domestic politics, regional alliances, humanitarian concerns, and international relations intricately intertwine to impact the decisions and actions of Arab states with regard to this long-standing conflict. An in-depth understanding of these factors is crucial for comprehending the complexities of the conflict and predicting the future course of action forArab states. Let's explore some additional factors that shape their influence on the Gaza conflict:

Religious and Cultural Factors:

Religious and cultural factors also play a significant role in shaping Arab states' approach to the Israeli-Palestinian conflict. The connection between the Palestinian cause and Islam makes the conflict deeply rooted in religious sentiment. The Al-Aqsa Mosque in Jerusalem, one of the holiest sites in Islam, holds great religious and symbolic significance for Muslims around the world, including Arab states. This religious connection fuels support and solidarity for the Palestinian cause among Arab populations, putting pressure on their respective governments to take a strong stance against Israeli policies.

Furthermore, cultural ties and historical legacies also shape Arab states' positions on the conflict. Arab societies often have a collective memory of past conflicts and grievances related to the Israeli-Palestinian issue, which influences their perspectives and narratives around the conflict. This historical and cultural context often fuels a sense of identity and solidarity with the Palestinian people, further shaping Arab states' policies and actions.

Security Concerns:

Security concerns also factor into Arab states' approach to the Israeli-Palestinian conflict. The instability and tensions caused by the conflict pose risks to the security of Arab states, including the potential for spillover effects, such as violence and extremism spreading beyond the conflict zone. This concern is particularly relevant for states sharing borders with Palestine, such as Jordan and Egypt, which have experienced the implications of the conflict firsthand.

Arab states recognise that the resolution of the Israeli-Palestinian conflict is crucial for the overall stability of the region. An unresolved conflict not only perpetuates violence but also creates an environment conducive to the spread of extremism and terrorism. Consequently, many Arab states view the resolution of the conflict as a means to enhance regional security and counter the threats they face.

geo-Political considerations:

Geopolitical considerations also factor into Arab states' approach to the Gaza conflict. Arab governments often have their own geopolitical priorities and strategic considerations that influence their stance on the conflict. This includes maintaining good relations with global powers, managing regional rivalries, or pursuing specific regional ambitions.

For example, countries like Saudi Arabia and the United Arab Emirates have increasingly prioritised countering Iran's influence in the region. This has led to a convergence of interests with Israel, as both countries share a common adversary in Iran and perceive Israel as a potential ally in this regard. Consequently, these states have taken a more pragmatic approach to the Israeli-Palestinian conflict, emphasising security cooperation with Israel over traditional solidarity with the Palestinians.

The geopolitical considerations of Arab states also extend to their relations with other regional players, such as Turkey and Iran. These states' involvement in the Israeli-Palestinian conflict, whether through supporting Hamas or advocating for Palestinian rights, can influence the positions and policies of Arab states, prompting them to take a more assertive or conservative approach depending on their geopolitical alignment.

Conclusion:

The Gaza conflict is a nuanced issue influenced by a multitude of socio-economic factors that shape Arab states' influence and approach to the conflict. Economic interests, domestic politics, regional alliances, humanitarian concerns, international relations, religious and cultural factors, security concerns, and geopolitical considerations all contribute to the complexities of the conflict. Understanding these factors is crucial for analysing the actions and policies of Arab states regarding Gaza and for predicting their future course of action. Ultimately, it underscores the need for a comprehensive and multifaceted approach to resolving the Israeli-Palestinian conflict.

Chapter 30

Geopolitical Considerations in the Israeli-Palestinian Conflict

T he Israeli-Palestinian conflict is not just a localised struggle; it holds significant geopolitical implications that reverberate throughout the region and the world. This chapter explores the geopolitical considerations that shape and influence the dynamics of this enduring conflict.

One of the primary geopolitical considerations in the Israeli-Palestinian conflict is the struggle for regional dominance. Various regional and global powers have vested interests in the outcome of this conflict, seeking to establish influence and control over the strategic Middle East region. The conflict serves as a battleground for power struggles between nations, as each seeks to gain the upper hand by aligning with either the Israeli or Palestinian side.

In the pursuit of regional dominance, countries such as Iran, Saudi

Arabia, Turkey, and Qatar have attempted to exploit the Israeli-Palestinian conflict. Iran, for example, has supported anti-Israeli militant groups like Hezbollah and Hamas, aiming to expand its influence in the region. It sees itself as the leader of the Islamic world and believes in the necessity of resisting Israeli control over Jerusalem, which holds significant religious and symbolic value for Muslims worldwide. Saudi Arabia and other Gulf states, on the other hand, have used their financial resources to exert influence over Palestinian factions. They often seek to gain support from Palestinian groups to promote their own interests and counter Iranian influence. These geopolitical manoeuvres exacerbate the conflict and fuel sectarian tensions, with consequences beyond the Israeli-Palestinian context.

In addition to the regional power struggle, the Israeli-Palestinian conflict is intertwined with broader regional security concerns. The actions and policies of both Israeli and Palestinian actors have implications for broader regional stability. The conflict has the potential to ignite further unrest and violence, leading to a destabilised Middle East. Therefore, regional powers often attempt to mediate or shape the conflict to safeguard their own security interests.

For instance, Egypt has historically played a crucial role in mediating between Israel and Palestine. Its efforts culminated in brokering the Camp David Accords in 1978, paving the way for the Israeli-Egyptian peace treaty. Egypt's involvement stems from its desire to ensure stability and security in its border region and mitigate potential challenges to its leadership in the Arab world. Additionally, Jordan, as a neighbouring state, also has a vested interest in the resolution of the conflict. It shares borders with both Israel and the West Bank, and any escalation in the conflict could have direct implications for its security and stability.

Another crucial geopolitical consideration is the influence of external actors. Countries outside the region, such as the United States, European Union, and several global powers, have their own strategic interests tied to the resolution of the Israeli-Palestinian conflict. These external actors have historically played key roles in peace processes and negotiations, often acting as mediators or facilitators. Their involvement can either help advance the prospects for a resolution or exacerbate the existing tensions.

The United States, for example, has traditionally been a significant player in efforts to resolve the Israeli-Palestinian conflict. Its motivations stem from its broad strategic interests in the Middle East, including ensuring stability, protecting allies, and promoting its own regional influence. Over the years, different U.S. administrations have taken varied approaches, with some being more actively involved in peace initiatives than others. The European Union, comprising 27 member states, is another influential actor seeking to promote peace and stability in its immediate neighbourhood. Europe's involvement is driven by its desire to protect its economic and security interests and prevent the spillover of conflict into its territory. However, external actors' involvement has not always yielded the desired results, in part due to competing interests and biased approaches.

Furthermore, the geographical and geopolitical factors of the conflict present unique challenges. The disputed territories, including the West Bank, Gaza Strip, and the status of Jerusalem, hold immense significance for both Israeli and Palestinian identity and sovereignty. Control over these territories involves control over valuable resources, security, and access to regional trade routes. The geopolitical importance of these territories adds another layer of complexity to the conflict, making it increasingly difficult to find a mutually acceptable compromise.

Additionally, neighbouring Arab states play a crucial role in the geopolitical considerations of the Israeli-Palestinian conflict. Arab countries, individually or collectively through the Arab League, have historically supported the Palestinian cause and exerted diplomatic pressure on Israel. Their support for Palestine is often driven by domestic and regional political considerations, including maintaining popular support and countering perceived Israeli aggression.

Nevertheless, the shifting regional dynamics and emerging alliances have led to evolving Arab state positions on the conflict. Some Arab states, such as the United Arab Emirates and Bahrain, have recently normalised their relations with Israel, prioritising their shared interests in countering Iran's influence and enhancing economic cooperation. This development significantly impacts the geopolitical landscape of the conflict and potentially reshapes alliances and power dynamics.

Moreover, the natural resources in the region also contribute to the geopolitical considerations. The discovery and extraction of significant offshore gas reserves in the Eastern Mediterranean have added a new dimension to the conflict. Israel, Cyprus, and Egypt have formed a cooperative energy triangle, aiming to exploit and export these resources. This cooperation has the potential to provide economic incentives for positive engagement between Israel and its neighbours while introducing new opportunities for regional cooperation.

Ultimately, the geopolitical considerations in the Israeli-Palestinian conflict highlight the interconnectedness of regional and international actors and their vested interests. The pursuit of power, security concerns, control over strategic territories, and access to resources all shape the dynamics of the conflict. As long as these geopolitical considerations persist, the path to a just and lasting resolution remains challenging.

Understanding these geopolitical factors is essential for comprehending the complexities of the Israeli-Palestinian conflict. Without acknowledging and addressing the broader regional context, any attempts at peace-building and reconciliation may fall short.

In the subsequent chapters, we will delve deeper into the roles of individual Arab states, external actors, the socio-economic factors, and the impact of natural resources, which further contribute to the geopolitics of this protracted conflict. By analysing the multidimensional aspects of the conflict, we can gain a more comprehensive understanding of the challenges and potential pathways towards a sustainable resolution.

Chapter 31

Conclusion and Reflections

I n this book, we have embarked on a profound and enlightening journey to understand the complexities of the Israeli-Palestinian conflict and the role that Arab states play in its resolution. Our exploration has delved into the intricate layers of historical context, examined the individual positions of 21 Arab states, and analysed the multifaceted challenges they face in achieving a lasting cease-fire. It is through this comprehensive examination that we have gained a deeper insight into this seemingly intractable conflict.

Throughout our analysis, it has become unequivocally clear that the Israeli-Palestinian conflict is deeply rooted in historical narratives and competing national aspirations. The struggle for land, identity, and self-determination has shaped the fundamental contours of this conflict. The intricate history shared between Israelis and Palestinians, defined by a complex interplay of colonialism, religious tensions, and competing claims to the land, has laid a formidable and highly resistant foundation for a protracted dispute.

Arab states, as neighbouring nations with shared cultural and religious ties to the Palestinian people, bear significant responsibility in contributing to the resolution of this longstanding conflict. However, they often find themselves constrained by a myriad of challenges. Chief among these is the fragmentation and diverging interests among Arab states themselves, which poses a formidable obstacle to forging a unified Arab stance on the Israeli-Palestinian conflict.

The diversity of visions, aspirations, and priorities within the Arab world, shaped by a range of factors including historical relationships, political dynamics, and internal challenges, further complicates efforts for collective action. Agreement and consensus on a common approach remain elusive, thereby limiting the efficacy of Arab states in influencing the trajectory of peace negotiations.

Such fragmentation is greatly exacerbated by the influence of external powers in the region. Global players like the United States, Russia, and the European Union have significant geopolitical and strategic interests at stake in the Middle East. Their involvement in the Israeli-Palestinian conflict often tilts the balance of power and shapes the outcomes of negotiations, sometimes overshadowing the voices and initiatives of Arab states. To truly advance the cause of peace, it is imperative to address these power dynamics and foster an inclusive environment that enables meaningful and balanced contributions from all stakeholders.

Additionally, economic and social factors play a significant role in determining Arab states' ability to engage effectively in the resolution of the Israeli-Palestinian conflict. Internal challenges, such as economic hardships, governance deficits, and demographic pressures, divert attention, resources, and political will away from addressing the conflict. Arab states must often prioritise their domestic concerns, hampering their capacity to actively contribute to mediation and reconciliation efforts.

To fully grasp the complexities at play, one must also delve into the intricate web of regional alliances and geopolitical considerations. Arab states' strategic positioning, influenced by historical enmities, shared ideologies, or geopolitical calculations, shapes their approach to the Israeli-Palestinian conflict. The regional power dynamics, such as the rivalry between Iran and Saudi Arabia, have spilt over into the conflict, further complicating the path to resolution. To navigate these complexities, it is essential to foster dialogue, build trust, and forge common ground among Arab states while considering the broader regional dynamics.

In conclusion, the Israeli-Palestinian conflict represents one of the most deeply rooted and complex issues of our time. Arab states, as critical stakeholders, face a multitude of obstacles on the path to achieving a just and lasting resolution. Overcoming the challenges of fragmentation, understanding the impact of external powers, addressing socio-economic factors, and navigating complex geopolitical considerations will be crucial steps towards finding a sustainable path to peace. This journey requires a comprehensive and nuanced understanding of the historical, political, economic, and social factors at play. It is our hope that this book has contributed to a more informed and enlightened discourse on the Israeli-Palestinian conflict, ultimately paving the way for a brighter and more harmonious future for all those impacted by this enduring struggle.

Chapter 32

References For Further Reading

The aim of the following list is to provide a diverse range of perspectives and deepen the understanding of the complex dynamics at play in the Israeli-Palestinian conflict and the role of Arab states.

Historical Context of the Israeli-Palestinian Conflict:

Pappe, Ilan. "The Ethnic Cleansing of Palestine." Oneworld Publications, 2006.
Morris, Benny. "1948: A History of the First Arab-Israeli War." Yale University Press, 2008.

Arab States' Individual Stances and Roles:

Barnett, Michael N. "Israel in the Middle East: The Complexity of the Arab State System." Columbia University Press, 2020.
Lynch, Marc. "The New Arab Wars: Uprisings and Anarchy in the

Middle East." Public Affairs, 2016.

Geopolitical Considerations in the Conflict:

Said, Edward W. "The Question of Palestine." Vintage, 1992.
Walt, Stephen M. "The Origins of Alliances." Cornell University Press, 1990.

Socio-economic Factors Impacting Arab States' Influence:

Roy, Sara. "Hamas and Civil Society in Gaza: Engaging the Islamist Social Sector." Princeton University Press, 2011.
Fawcett, Louise (ed.). "International Relations of the Middle East." Oxford University Press, 2019.

Marginalization of Arab States in the Conflict:

Khalidi, Rashid. "The Iron Cage: The Story of the Palestinian Struggle for Statehood." Beacon Press, 2007.
Gause, F. Gregory III. "Saudi Arabia in the New Middle East." Council on Foreign Relations Special Report, 2011.

Regional Dynamics and Political Landscape Influences:

Lesch, Ann M. and Tessler, Mark (eds.). "Israel, Egypt, and the Palestinians: From Camp David to Intifada." Indiana University Press, 2002.
Telhami, Shibley. "The World Through Arab Eyes: Arab Public Opinion and the Reshaping of the Middle East." Basic Books, 2013.

www.ingramcontent.com/pod-product-compliance
Lightning Source LLC
Chambersburg PA
CBHW072153270326
41930CB00011B/2404